Flowers *of the* BIBLE

By Helga Curtis

HOUSE of WHITE BIRCHES

Contents

Executive Editor: Jeanne Stauffer; **Associate Editor:** Dianne Schmidt;
Technical Editor: Mary Jo Kurten; **Technical Artists:** Liz Morgan,
Mitch Moss, Chad Summers; **Copy Editors:** Michelle Beck,
Nicki Lehman, Mary Martin; **Graphic Arts Supervisor:** Ronda Bechinski;
Graphic Artist: Erin Augsburger; **Photography:** Tammy Christian,
Christena Green, Kelly Heydinger; **Photography Stylist:** Tammy Nussbaum

ISBN: 978-1-59217-012-8
Library of Congress number: 2002113547
5 6 7 8 9 10 11

FLOWERS OF THE BIBLE is published by House of White Birches,
306 East Parr Road, Berne, IN 46711. Printed in USA. Copyright © 2003
House of White Birches.

RETAIL STORES: If you would like to carry this pattern book or any
other DRG publications, visit DRGwholesale.com.

Every effort has been made to ensure that the instructions in this
pattern book are complete and accurate. We cannot, however, take responsibility
for human error, typographical mistakes or variations in individual work. Please
visit ClotildeCustomerCare.com to check for pattern updates.

Introduction

There has been a concentrated effort by many scholars, especially those who are expert in Semitic languages, to correctly identify biblical plants and flowers. Some, according to the experts, will be in limbo forever.

The Bible has been translated time and time again. The English and other European botanical translations are not good.

Early and later translations were unfortunately not versed in floral terms of original Hebrew scripture. The translators have hardly any scientific value, but are historically important.

It has been established that "flowers or lilies of the field" could embrace at least ten different species. Matthew 6:28–30 mentions the lilies of the field, but it is now believed the lily in this instance was the red crown anemone, which grows wild.

There are 110 plants mentioned in the Bible. Some are referred to a hundred times over and others less often and some only once. About 18 of the species are not named accurately because the narrator was more interested in their importance than in their correct name. Hence, we have a reoccurrence of the term "lilies of the field." For instance, there are 20 names for thorns in the Bible. Some plant names were given to more than one plant species.

Isaiah had the richest vocabulary of plant names, some of which may never be recognized. Listed among the field flowers is the common red poppy, which grows between the grain to be harvested, and the narcissus, also known as the sea daffodil. It is believed that the narcissus was the biblical lily, but is actually a member of the amaryllis family.

Poppies, chamomiles, tulips, narcissi, crowfoots, tulips and anemones provide spectacular displays throughout Israel during spring and summer, and in the Old Testament they symbolize the ephemeral nature of things in contrast to the ever-enduring word of God.

—*Helga Curtis*

The voice said, Cry. And he said, What shall I cry?
All flesh is grass, and all the goodliness thereof is as the flower of the field:
The grass withereth, the flower fadeth:
because the spirit of the LORD bloweth upon it: surely the people is grass.
The grass withereth, the flower fadeth: but the word of our God shall stand for ever.
—Isaiah 40:6–8

Lentil

Then Jacob gave Esau bread and a pottage of lentils: and he did eat and drink, and rose up, and went his way: thus Esau despised his birthright.
—Genesis 25:34

The lentil is just as important as a crop today as it was during biblical times. It is still used as a bread ingredient as well as for pottage, a thick soup or stew.

Esau, the elder twin brother of very jealous Jacob, came home from a journey, faint with hunger. He begged his brother for some bread and lentil pottage. Jacob shared, but with a stipulation. Esau was to give up his birthright, which he did.

Lentil
14 1/2" x 14 1/2" Block

Project Specifications
Wall Quilt Size: 16 1/2" x 16 1/2"

Fabric & Batting
- Neutral background square 16" x 16"
- 4 medium blue print border strips 1 1/2" x 17 1/2"
- Variety of green, aqua and blue scraps for appliqué
- 2 yards purchased or self-made medium blue binding
- Backing 20" x 20"
- Batting 20" x 20"

Supplies & Tools
- Template material of choice
- Appliqué thread of choice to match fabrics
- All-purpose thread to blend with fabrics
- Medium green 6-strand embroidery floss
- Embroidery needle
- 1 spool natural quilting thread

Instructions
1. Referring to photo for color suggestions, prepare templates and fabric for appliqué method of choice. Appliqué pieces on background square.
2. With 2 strands of medium green 6-strand embroidery floss, embroider tendrils at ends of leaves with stem stitch as shown on patterns.
3. Trim background square to 15" x 15 ". Add border strips, mitering corners as in General Instructions. Trim to square.
4. Layer backing, batting and block, and baste. Quilt as desired.
5. Bind quilt to finish. ✱

Center

Lentil
Left

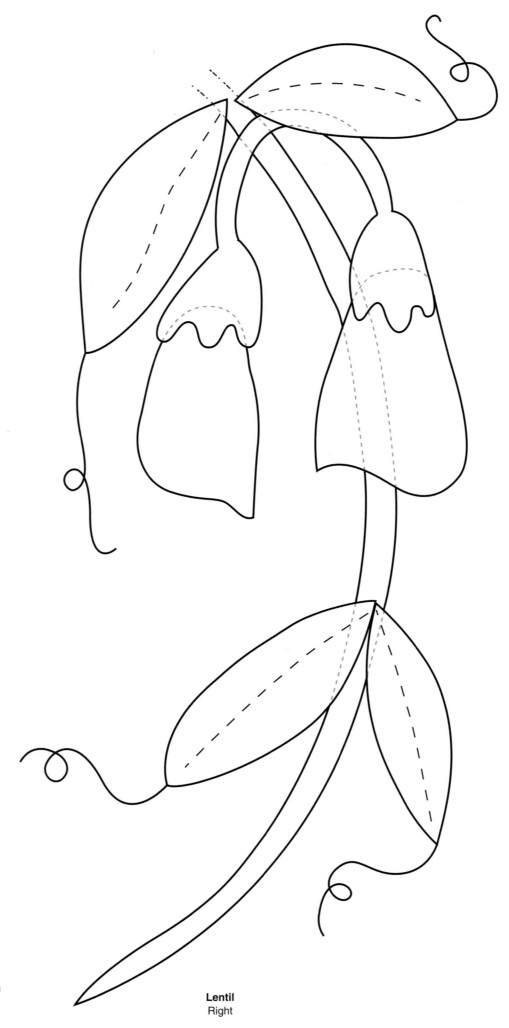

Lentil
Right

Lentil
Top

Mandrake

And Reuben went in the days of wheat harvest, and found mandrakes in the field, and brought them unto his mother Leah. Then Rachel said to Leah, Give me, I pray thee, of thy son's mandrakes.
—Genesis 30:14

The Mandrake is referred to in Hebrew as the "love apple."

The rugged root, which resembles the lower part of the body, struck superstitious terror into people throughout the ages.

Because of the root's formation, it was known as an aphrodisiac. It supposedly excited voluptuousness and induced fertility. In the Bible, one can read about Leah and Rachel, who used the fruit to induce fertility.

Mandrake is of the nightshade family and related to the potato and tomato. It is also reported that eaten to excess, it can cause insanity. It can also cause death. Jews considered the plant a charm against evil.

King Henry VIII sold mandrake charms during his reign.

Mandrake
16" x 16 Block

Project Specifications

Size: 20" x 20"

Fabric & Batting

- Neutral background square 17 1/2" x 17 1/2"
- 1/4 yard light green print for inner and outer borders
- 1/4 yard multicolored batik for center border
- Light bluish-lavender batik, rose batik, yellow and variety of green prints for appliqué
- 2 1/2 yards purchased or self-made binding
- Backing 24" x 24"
- Batting 24" x 24"

Supplies & Tools

- Template material of choice
- Appliqué thread of choice to match fabrics
- All-purpose thread to blend with fabrics
- Lavender, green and white 6-strand embroidery floss
- Embroidery needle
- 1 spool natural quilting thread

Instructions

1. Referring to photo for color suggestions, prepare templates and fabric for appliqué method of choice. Appliqué pieces on background square.

2. With 3 strands of green embroidery floss, embroider veins on leaves with stem stitch as shown on patterns.

3. With 2 strands of lavender embroidery floss, work stem stitch on flowers as shown on pattern.

4. Referring to Figure 1 and using white 6-strand embroidery floss,

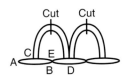

Figure 1
Cut loops as shown to make fringe.

make several stitches at the center of the flower, bringing thread up at A, down at B, etc., and making loops approximately 1/2" long. Cut the loops open, again referring to Figure 1 to make a fringelike flower center.

5. Trim background square to 16 1/2" x 16 1/2".

6. From light green print cut four strips each 1 1/4" x 22" and 1" x 22". From multicolored batik cut four strips 1 1/4" x 22". Sew one batik strip between a 1"- and 1 1/2"-wide light green strip. Press seams toward green borders. Handle each as a single border and sew to center square as in General Instructions. Miter corners. Trim to square.

7. Layer backing, batting and block, and baste. Quilt as desired.

8. Bind quilt to finish. ✳

Mandrake
Bottom

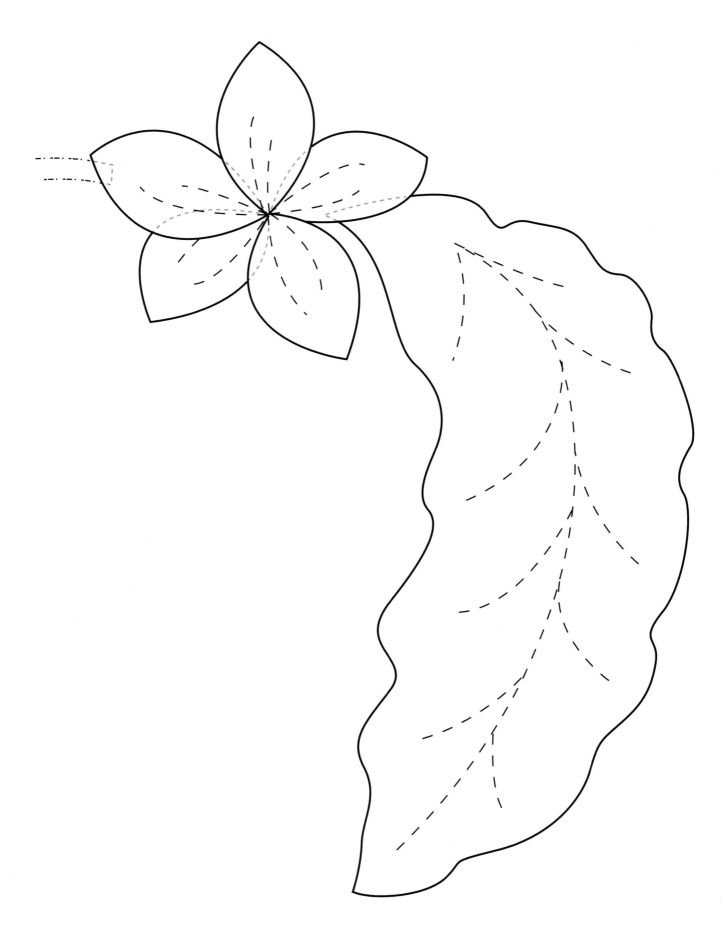

Mandrake
Right

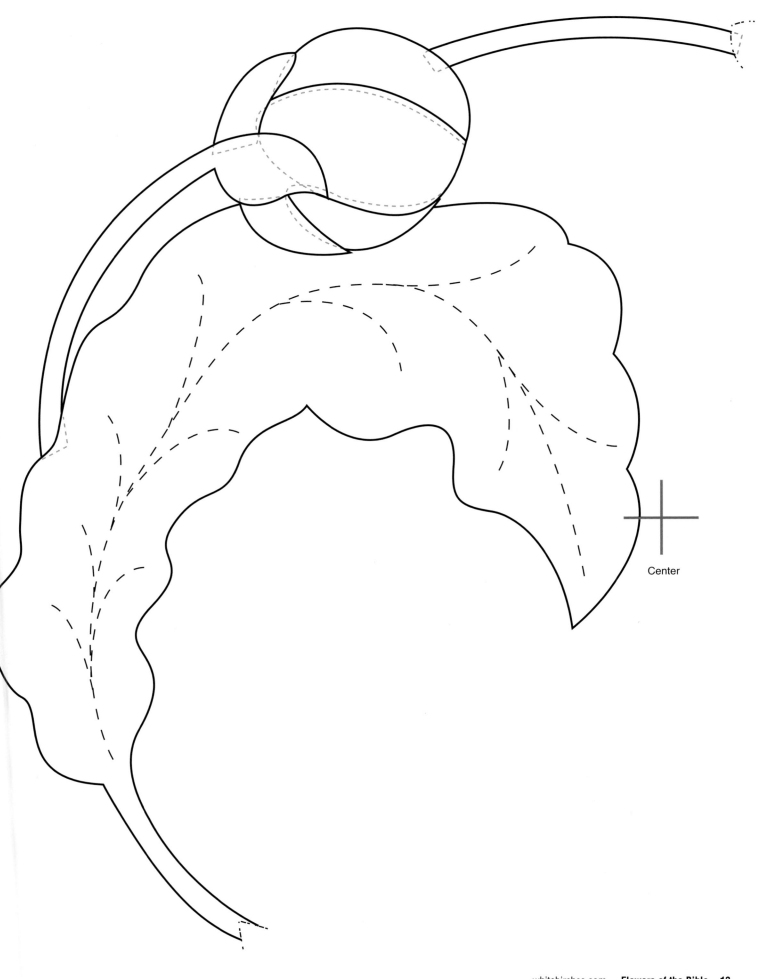

Center

Balm

Balm was known in the trade long before it was mentioned in the Bible. It is believed that the Queen of Sheba (Makeda) brought the balm plant to King Solomon. The use was threefold, as a holy oil, healing agent and antidote for snakebite. It was also used as an ingredient of perfume.

The kingdom of Sheba was believed to have been founded by Shem, a son of Noah, at the heel of the Saudi Arabian boot, across from Ethiopia. The queen had heard about the fame of Solomon and ventured north to see his accomplishments. She came to Jerusalem with a great train of camels bearing gifts of gold, gems and balm.

At the time of Makeda's visit, Solomon was at the peak of his power and they probably discussed and negotiated commercial agreements. Israel stood at the center of land routes between Asia and Africa, and its ports linked the Red Sea, the Atlantic and Mediterranean.

Yelsak, a 14th century monk wrote that the Queen of Sheba was impregnated by Solomon. She delivered a son and converted to Judaism. Haile Selassie claimed to be a result of this union.

Although very little is said about the queen, her memory was kept alive with folklore and traditional stories. Shem is now Yemen.

The children of Eastern lands spend their coins for this material, which they chew like gum.

Balm
15" x 15" Block

Project Specifications
Size: 16 1/2" x 16 1/2"

Fabric & Batting
- Neutral background square 16 1/2" x 16 1/2"
- 4 border strips 1 1/4" x 18"
- Scraps of rust-and-green print and a variety of green scraps for appliqué
- 2 yards purchased or self-made binding
- Backing 20" x 20"
- Batting 20" x 20"

Supplies & Tools
- Template material of choice
- Appliqué thread of choice to match fabrics
- All-purpose thread to blend with fabrics
- Black and green 6-strand embroidery floss

- Embroidery needle
- 1 spool natural quilting thread

Instructions

1. Referring to photo for color suggestions, prepare templates and fabric for appliqué method of choice. Appliqué pieces on background square.

2. With 2 strands of green 6-strand embroidery floss, embroider veins on leaves with running stitch as shown on patterns.

3. With 2 strands of black 6-strand embroidery floss, work stem stitch lines around the blossom as shown on pattern. Work a French knot at the end of each line.

4. Trim background square to 15 1/2" x 15 1/2". Add border strips, mitering corners as in General Instructions. Trim to square.

5. Layer backing, batting and block, and baste. Quilt as desired.

6. Bind quilt to finish. ✳

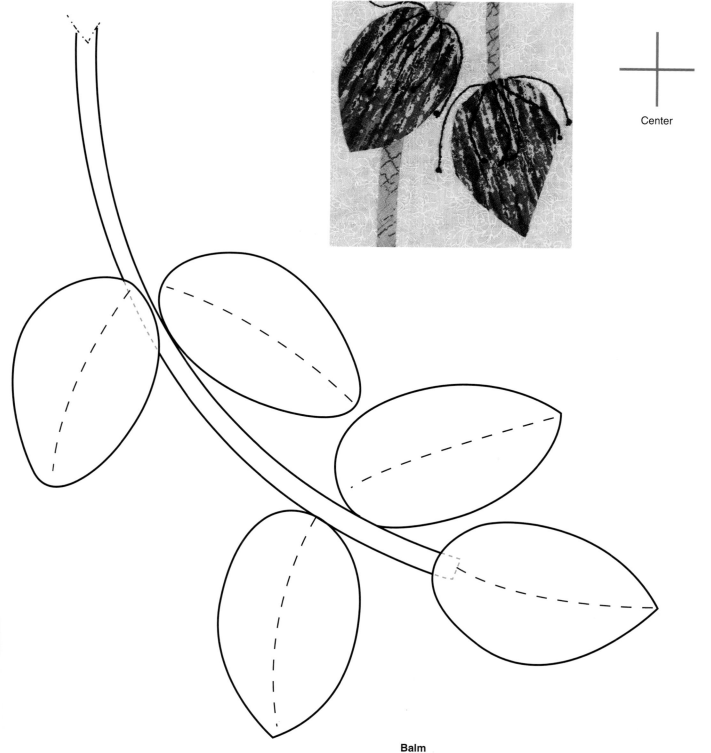

Center

Balm
Left

Leaf Placement

Balm
Right

Balm
Top

Rock Rose

And their father Israel said unto them, If it must be so now, do this; take of the best fruits in the land in your vessels, and carry down the man a present, a little balm, and a little honey, spices, and myrrh, nuts and almonds.

—Genesis 43:11

The myrrh of Genesis is probably not the true myrrh, but rather the gum exuded by a species of the Rock Rose, called ladanum. Today, herdsmen send their goats through the plants and then comb the gum out of their beards. This plant grows amongst the rocks.

The gift of myrrh at the time of Christ's birth designated the hardship and suffering he would endure.

Rock Rose
15" x 15" Block

Project Specifications

Wall Quilt Size: 17 1/2" x 17 1/2"

Fabric & Batting

- Neutral background square 16 1/2" x 16 1/2"
- 4 dark red border strips 1 3/4" x 18 1/2"
- Variety of red, green and gold scraps for appliqué
- 2 1/4 yards purchased or self-made dark green binding
- Backing 21" x 21"
- Batting 21" x 21"

Supplies & Tools

- Template material of choice
- Appliqué thread of choice to match fabrics
- All-purpose thread to blend with fabrics
- Gold and green 6-strand embroidery floss
- Embroidery needle
- 1 spool natural quilting thread

Instructions

1. Referring to photo for color suggestions, prepare templates and fabric for appliqué method of choice. Appliqué pieces on background square.

2. With 2 strands of green 6-strand embroidery floss, embroider veins on leaves with stem stitch as shown on patterns.

3. With 2 strands of gold 6-strand embroidery floss, work a straight stitch around the flower center, placing a French knot at the end of each stitch as shown in Figure 1. Fill flower center with French knots.

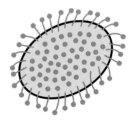

Figure 1
Work embroidery stitches and French knots around flower center as shown.

4. Trim background square to 15 1/2" x 15 1/2". Add border strips, mitering corners as in General Instructions. Trim to square.

5. Layer backing, batting and block, and baste. Quilt as desired.

6. Bind quilt to finish. ✳

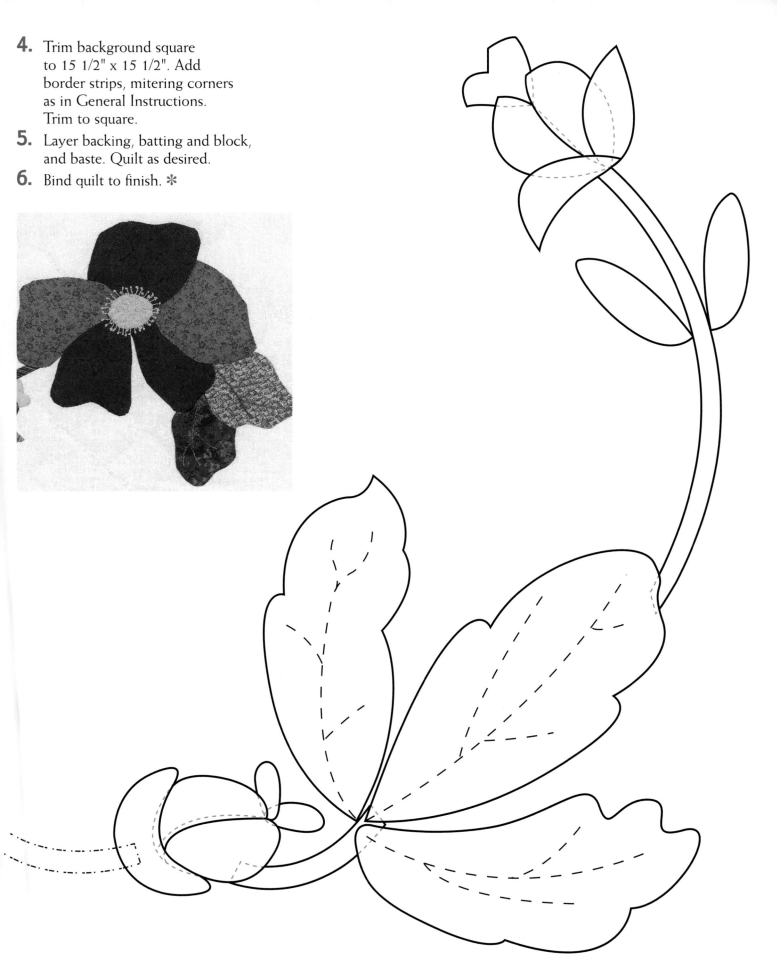

Rock Rose
Right

Center

Rock Rose
Left

Rock Rose
Top

Cattails

And when she could not longer hide him, she took for him an ark of bulrushes, and daubed it with slime and with pitch, and put the child therein; and she laid it in the flags by the river's brink.
—Exodus 2:3
—Also Isaiah 19:6 and Jonah 2:5

There is an old painting depicting Jesus sitting at a mock trial with a cattail in his hand as a scepter.

The sweet and soft marrow of the immature spike is considered a delicacy. The ashes are used as a salt substitute.

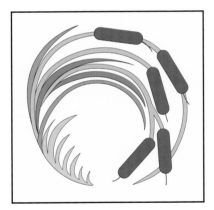

Cattails
15" x 15" Block

Project Specifications
Size: 19 3/4" x 19 3/4"

Fabric & Batting
- Neutral background square 16 1/2" x 16 1/2"
- 1/4 yard beige print for middle border

- 1/2 yard brown print for inner and outer borders and cattails
- Green and beige prints for appliqué
- 2 1/2 yards purchased or self-made binding
- Backing 24" x 24"
- Batting 24" x 24"

Supplies & Tools
- Template material of choice
- Appliqué thread of choice to match fabrics
- All-purpose thread to blend with fabrics
- Brown 6-strand embroidery floss
- Embroidery needle
- 1 spool natural quilting thread

Instructions
1. Referring to photo for color suggestions, prepare templates and fabric for appliqué method of choice. Appliqué pieces on background square.
2. With 3 strands of brown 6-strand embroidery floss and stem stitch, embroider the lines indicated at the end of each cattail spike.
3. Trim background square to 15 1/2" x 15 1/2".
4. From brown print cut eight strips 1 1/4" x 22". From beige print cut four strips 1 3/8" x 22". Sew one beige strip between two brown strips. Press seams toward brown borders. Handle each as a single border and sew to center square. Miter corners as in General Instructions and trim to square.
5. Layer backing, batting and block, and baste. Quilt as desired.
6. Bind quilt to finish. ✷

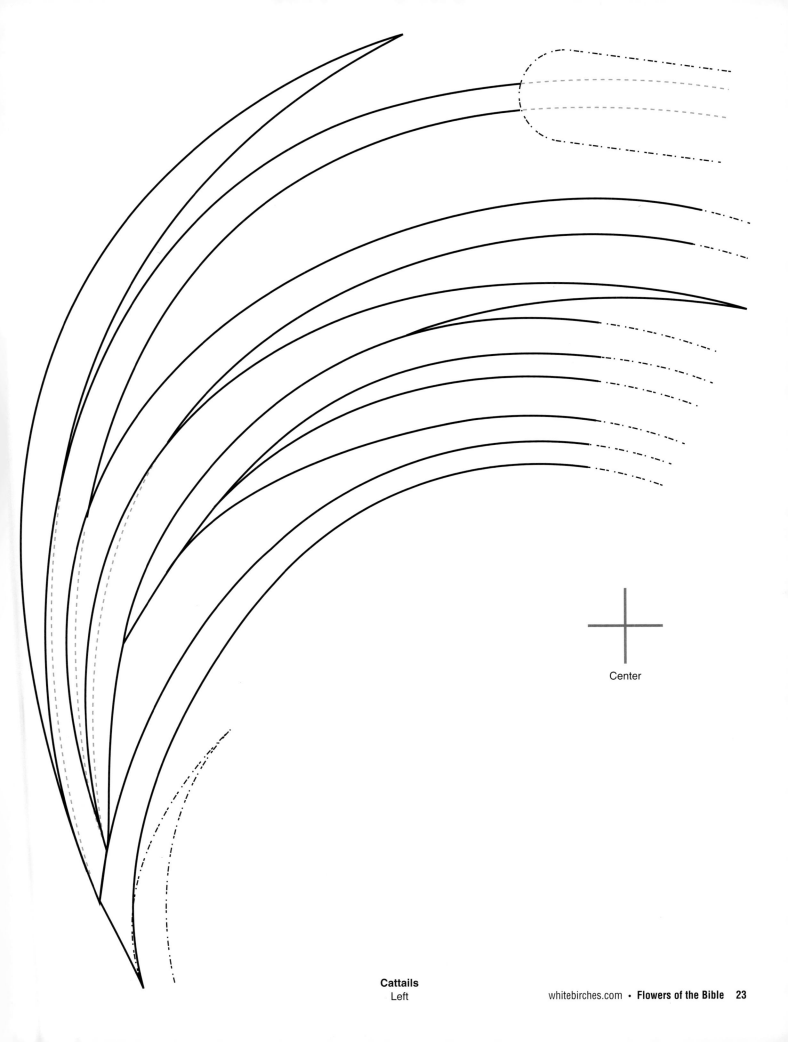

Cattails
Left

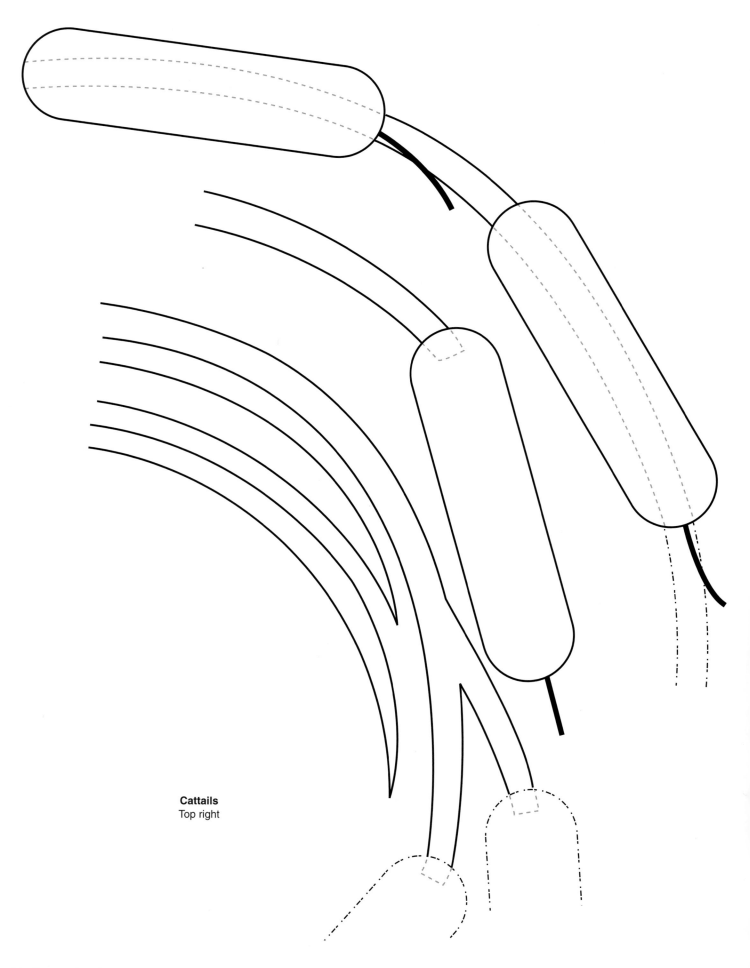

Cattails
Top right

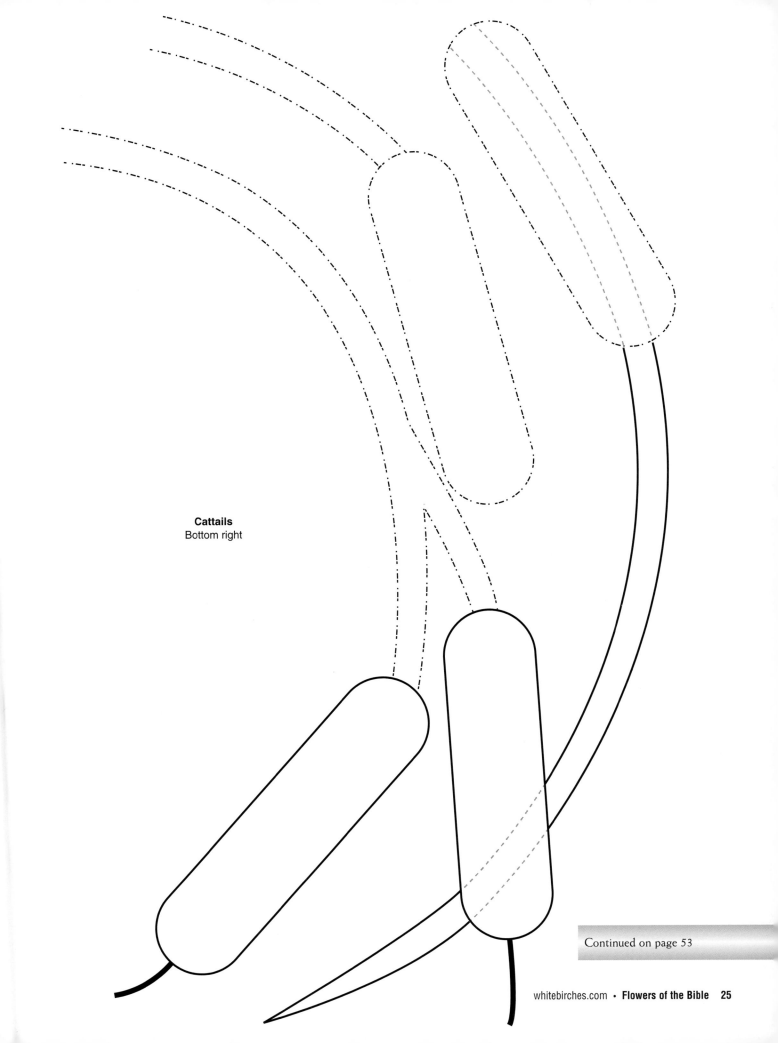

Cattails
Bottom right

Continued on page 53

Coriander

And the house of Israel called the name thereof Manna: and it was like coriander seed, white; and the taste of it was like wafers made with honey.

—Exodus 16:31

Coriander is one of the oldest herbs known to mankind. The plant was used for culinary and medical purposes by Hippocrates in 1440 B.C.

This plant grows well in Egypt and Israel. The young plant is known as cilantro.

Coriander seeds were prescribed as an anti-flatulent. If eaten to excess they have the harmful effect of a narcotic.

In *The Thousand and One Nights* coriander was used as an aphrodisiac.

Both seeds and leaves are highly aromatic. Dried, they combine the taste of lemon peel and sage.

Coriander
15" x 15" Block

Project Specifications

Size: 20" x 20"

Fabric & Batting

- Neutral background square 16 1/2" x 16 1/2"
- 1/4 yard green print for inner and outer borders and appliqué
- 1/4 yard gold solid for middle border and appliqué
- Scraps of white, green, pink and brown for appliqué
- 2 1/2 yards purchased or self-made binding
- Backing 24" x 24"
- Batting 24" x 24"

Supplies & Tools

- Template material of choice
- Appliqué thread of choice to match fabrics
- All-purpose thread to blend with fabrics
- Pink 6-strand embroidery floss
- Embroidery needle
- 1 spool natural quilting thread

Instructions

1. Referring to photo for color suggestions, prepare templates and fabric for appliqué method of choice. Appliqué pieces on background square.

2. With 3 strands of pink embroidery floss, work six French knots in pink flower center.

3. Trim background square to 15 1/2" x 15 1/2".

4. From green print cut eight strips 1 3/8" x 22". From gold solid cut four strips 1 1/4" x 22". Sew one gold strip between two green strips. Press seams toward green borders. Handle each as a single border and sew to center square. Miter corners as in General Instructions and trim to square.

5. Layer backing, batting and block, and baste. Quilt as desired.

6. Bind quilt to finish. ✱

Coriander
Top right

Center

Coriander
Bottom left

Coriander
Top left

Coriander
Bottom right

Flax

Moreover thou shalt make the tabernacle with ten curtains of fine twined linen, and blue, and purple, and scarlet: with cherubims of cunning work shalt thou make them.
—Exodus 26:1

And they made coats of fine linen of woven work for Aaron, and for his sons.
And a mitre of fine linen, and goodly bonnets of fine linen, and linen breeches of fine twined linen.
And a girdle of fine twined linen, and blue, and purple, and scarlet, of needlework; as the LORD commanded Moses.
—Exodus 39:27–29

Linen, which is made from flax, is one of the oldest textiles. It has been carbon-dated to 9,000 years ago. Pharaohs were bound in linen so fine it cannot be duplicated today.

Flax
16" x 16" Block

There are 52 references in the Bible referring to flax (linen).

There were three distinct types of linen worn during biblical times. The ordinary is mentioned in Daniel 10:5, Ezekial 9:2 and Revelation 15:6. The second type was superior and referred to in Exodus 26:1 and 39:29. The third, a linen of finest quality and costliest mentioned in Esther 8:15, I Chronicles 15:27 and Revelation 19:8.

The finest artist canvasses are made of linen as well as linseed oil used in painting.

Linen is more durable than silk and three times stronger than cotton. Early rugs were replaced in 1860 by linoleum (lin meaning flax and olem meaning oil).

Flax seeds are 24 percent protein, prescribed as a demulcent, emollient and laxative. The seeds were also used to prevent breast and colon cancer.

Project Specifications
Size: 21" x 21"

Fabric & Batting
- Neutral background square 16 1/2" x 16 1/2"
- 1/4 yard blue print for inner border, binding and appliqué
- 3/8 yard medium blue solid for inner and outer borders, binding and appliqué
- Green, blue, lavender and gold scraps for appliqué
- Backing 25" x 25"
- Batting 25" x 25"

Supplies & Tools
- Template material of choice
- Appliqué thread of choice to match fabrics
- All-purpose thread to blend with fabrics
- 1 spool natural quilting thread

Instructions
1. Referring to photo for color

suggestions, prepare templates and fabric for appliqué method of choice. Appliqué pieces on background square.

2. Trim background square to 16 1/2" x 16 1/2".

3. From medium blue solid cut four strips each 1" x 22" and 1 1/2" x 22". From blue print cut four strips 1 1/2" x 22". Sew one blue print strip between a 1"- and a 1 1/2"-wide blue solid strip. Press seams toward blue print borders. Handle each piece as a single border and sew to center square as in General Instructions. Miter corners. Trim to square.

4. Piece 2 1/2"-wide strips of blue solid and blue print together, alternating colors and varying lengths for a multicolored binding.

5. Layer backing, batting and block, and baste. Quilt as desired.

6. Bind quilt to finish. ✳

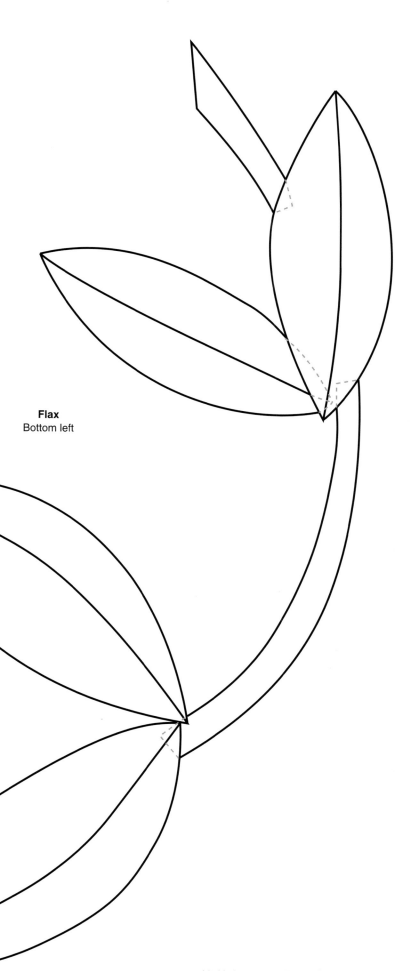

Flax
Bottom left

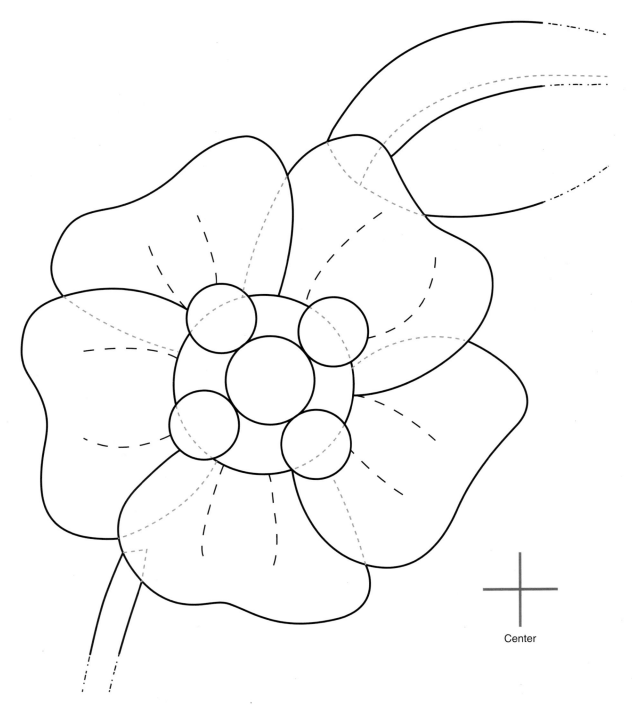

Flax
Top left

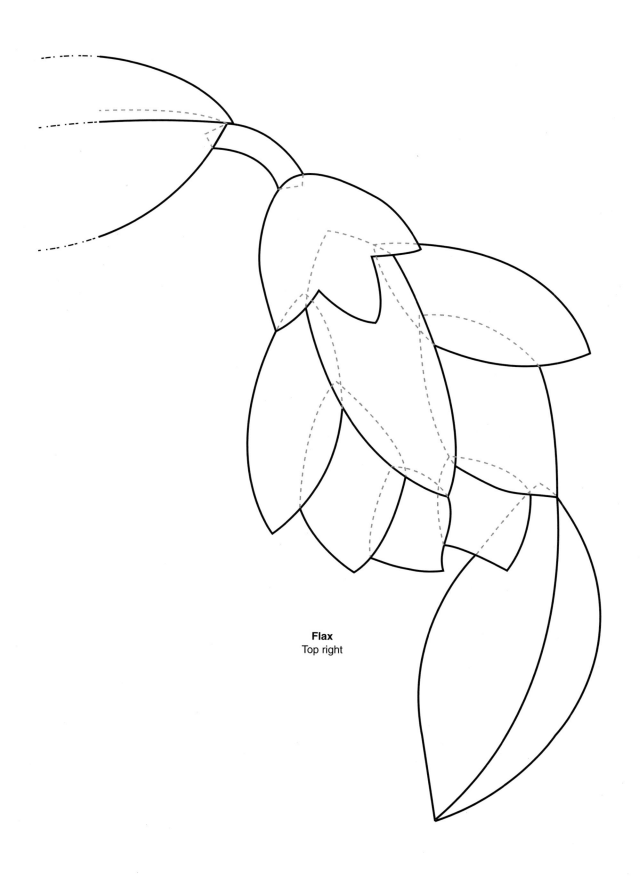

Flax
Top right

Frankincense

*And the LORD said unto Moses,
Take unto thee sweet spices, stacte,
and onycha and galbanum; these
sweet spices, with pure frankincense:
of each shall there be a like weight:
And thou shalt make it a perfume,
a confection after the art of the
apothecary, tempered together, pure
and holy.*
—*Exodus 30:34—35*
—*Also Matthew 2:10—11*

The gift of frankincense acknowl-
edges the holiness or divinity at
the time of Christ's birth.

Frankincense is an important
ingredient of incense. Today,
it is still used in high-grade
perfumes, especially in oriental
and floral types such as Mennon
Millionaire, Sculptura by Jovan
and Volcan D'Amour by Diane
von Furstenburg.

The meaning of frankincense is:

frank: free

incense: lightening

Frankincense
16" x 16" Block

Project Specifications

Size: 20" x 20"

Fabric & Batting

- Neutral background square
  17 1/2" x 17 1/2"
- 1/4 yard yellow print for center
  border and appliqué stem
- 3/8 yard medium green print
  for inner and outer borders and
  some leaves
- Green and white scraps for
  appliqué
- 2 1/2 yards purchased or
  self-made green binding
- Backing 24" x 24"
- Batting 24" x 24"

Supplies & Tools

- Template material of choice
- Appliqué thread of choice to
  match fabrics
- All-purpose thread to blend
  with fabrics
- Red 6-strand embroidery floss
- Embroidery needle
- 1 spool natural quilting thread

Instructions

1. Referring to photo for color
   suggestions, prepare templates
   and fabric for appliqué method
   of choice. Appliqué pieces on
   background square.

2. For gathered blossoms, trace
   19 circles on white fabric
   using a quarter (25 cents) as a
   template. Leave at least 1/2"
   between circles. Place traced
   circles on a second piece
   of white fabric, right sides
   facing. Cut out the circles
   1/4" outside the traced line
   through both layers of fabric

as shown in Figure 1. Repeat for 19 circle sets.

side out through the slits and make four marks as shown in Figure 3. Repeat for all 19 circles.

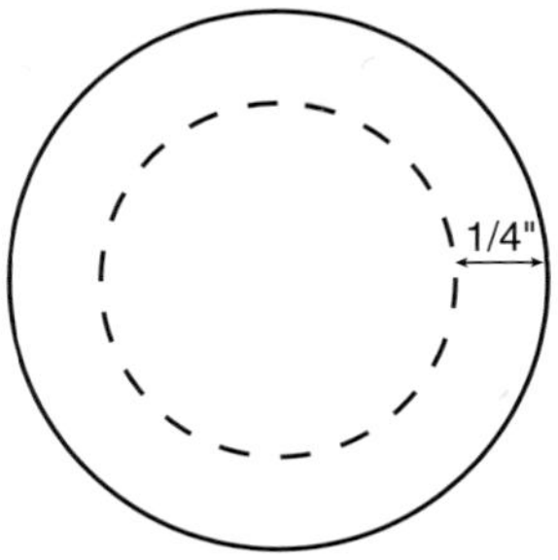

Figure 1
Cut circles 1/4" outside traced line.

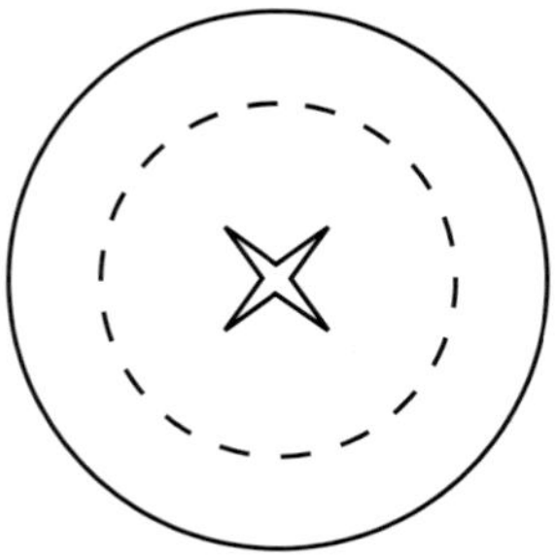

Figure 2
Cut a small X at the center of one layer of circle.

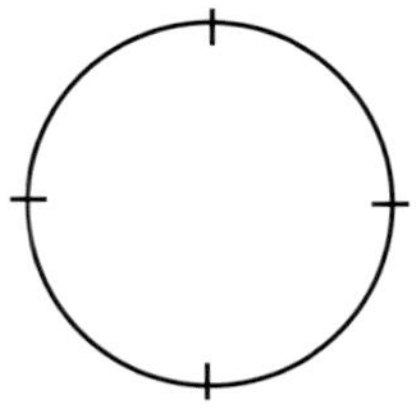

Figure 3
Turn circles right side out and mark 4 places as shown.

1/4"

Center

3. Sew a running stitch on the traced line. Knot at both ends but do not gather the thread. Carefully cut a small X in the center of one circle as shown in Figure 2. Turn the circles right

Frankincense
Left

4. With knotted white all-purpose thread, come up through the center of the circle. Wrap the thread over the mark at the top of the circle and bring the needle up again at the center. Pull the thread up tight and knot as shown in Figure 4, but do not cut. Repeat at each of the marks, working around the circle clockwise. This will create a four-petal flower as shown in Figure 5.

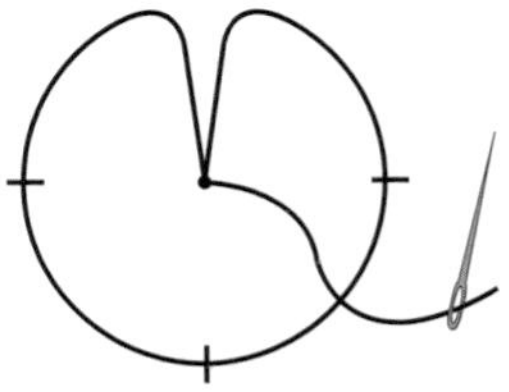

Figure 4
Pull thread up tight and knot as shown.

Figure 5
4-petal flower.

Frankincense
Right

Frankincense
Top

5. With white all-purpose thread, tack flowers in place as shown on pattern.

6. With 3 strands of red 6-strand embroidery floss, make three French knots at the center of each blossom.

7. Trim background square to 16 1/2" x 16 1/2".

8. From medium green print cut four strips each 1 1/4" x 22" and 1" x 22". From yellow print cut four strips 1 1/4" x 22". Sew one yellow strip between a 1"- and 1 1/2"-wide green strip. Press seams toward green borders. Handle each as a single border and sew to center square with narrower green border next to center square. Miter corners as in General Instructions. Trim to square.

9. Layer backing, batting and block, and baste. Quilt as desired.

10. Bind quilt to finish. ✳

Grapevine

And Noah began to be a husband-man, and he planted a vineyard.
—Genesis 9:20

A land of wheat, and barley, and vines, and fig trees, and pomegranates; a land of olive oil and honey;
—Deuteronomy 8:8

Binding his foal unto the vine, and his ass's colt unto the choice vine; he washed his garments in wine, and his clothes in the blood of grapes.
—Genesis 49:11

I am the true vine, and my Father is the husbandman.
—John 15:1

The grapevine, wheat and olive were essentials to all in the Holy Lands. Very often, in countries where water was not too abundant, wine was used to quench thirst. Palestine natives used the white grape for wine. The grape was fermented and contained alcohol. Because of climatic conditions, the natives could not keep grape juice fresh longer than two days.

According to Deuteronomy, Palestine was the promised land. Vines of Palestine were known for their heavy clusters of very large, juicy grapes. It is believed that Moses sent spies to explore the land of Canaan, and they cut a cluster of grapes so large it took two men to hold them on a staff. Botanists believe the first vine came from Armenia.

The fruitful vine brought out of Egypt symbolized the Jewish people. Jesus compared himself with the true vine and his disciples were the branches.

The story most of us are familiar with is that Noah planted the first vineyard after the flood. After imbibing in his own produce, Noah is recorded as the first drunkard. Too bad he didn't abide by the Talmud, which advises that women should only have one glass of wine and more would lead to embarrassment.

Project Specifications

Wall Quilt Size: 19" x 19"

Fabric & Batting

- Neutral background square 16" x 16"
- 1/8 yard green-and-lavender print for inner border and appliqué
- 1/8 yard light green print for center border and appliqué
- 1/4 yard medium green print for outer border and appliqué
- Scraps of marbled purple for appliqué
- 2 1/4 yards purchased or self-made purple binding

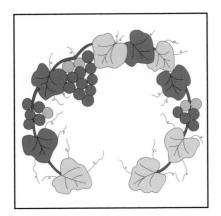

Grapevine
14 1/2" x 14 1/2" Block

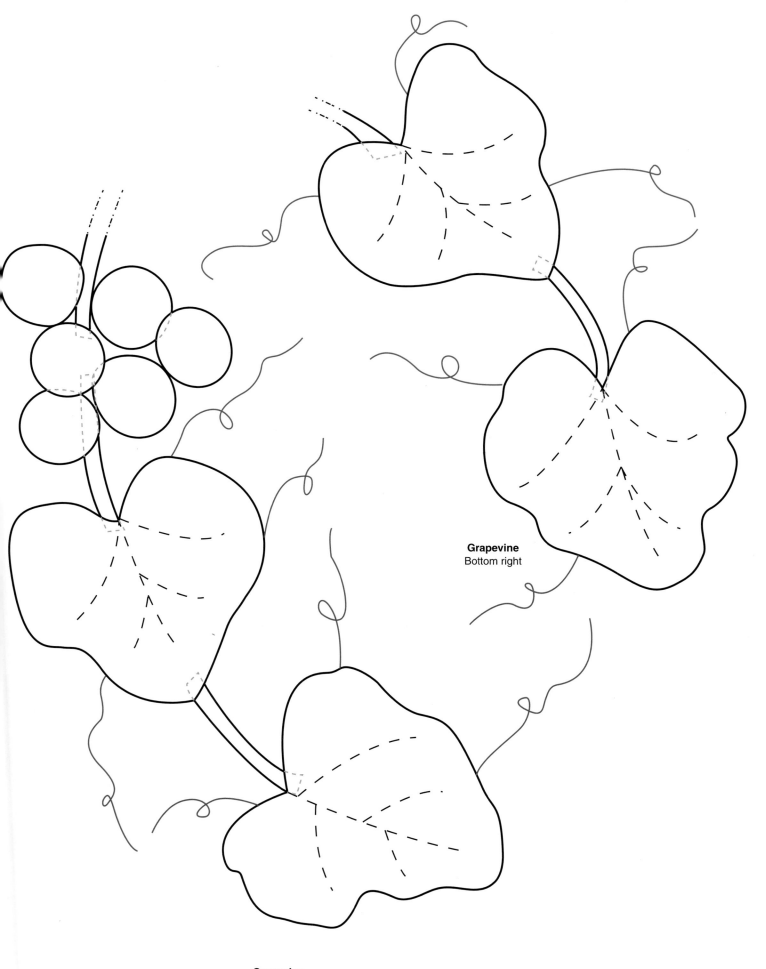

Grapevine
Bottom right

Grapevine
Bottom left

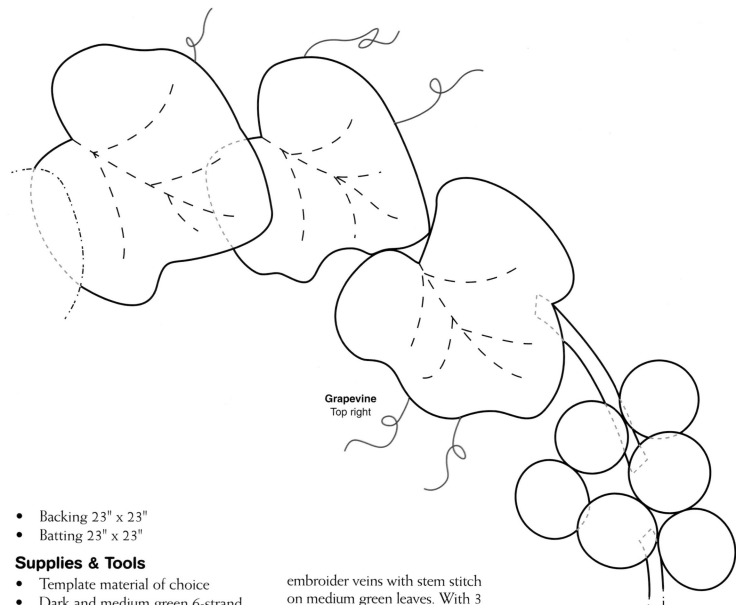

Grapevine
Top right

- Backing 23" x 23"
- Batting 23" x 23"

Supplies & Tools

- Template material of choice
- Dark and medium green 6-strand embroidery floss
- Appliqué thread of choice to match fabrics
- All-purpose thread to blend with fabrics
- Red, green and natural quilting threads

Instructions

1. Referring to photo for color suggestions, prepare templates and fabric for appliqué method of choice. Appliqué pieces on background square.

2. With 3 strands of dark green 6-strand embroidery floss embroider veins with stem stitch on medium green leaves. With 3 strands of medium green 6-strand embroidery floss, embroider veins with stem stitch on light green leaves and tendrils as shown on pattern. Work close buttonhole stitch around edges of all leaves.

3. Trim background square to 15" x 15".

4. Cut four strips each 1" x 22" from green-and-lavender print and light green print. From medium green print cut four strips 1 3/4" x 22". Sew one light green print strip between a medium green print strip and green-and-lavender print strip. Repeat for four borders. Press seams toward outer border. Handle each piece as a single border and sew to center square as in General Instructions, lavender-and-green print border nearest appliquéd block. Miter corners. Trim to square.

5. Layer backing, batting and block, and baste. Quilt as desired.

6. Bind quilt to finish. ✳

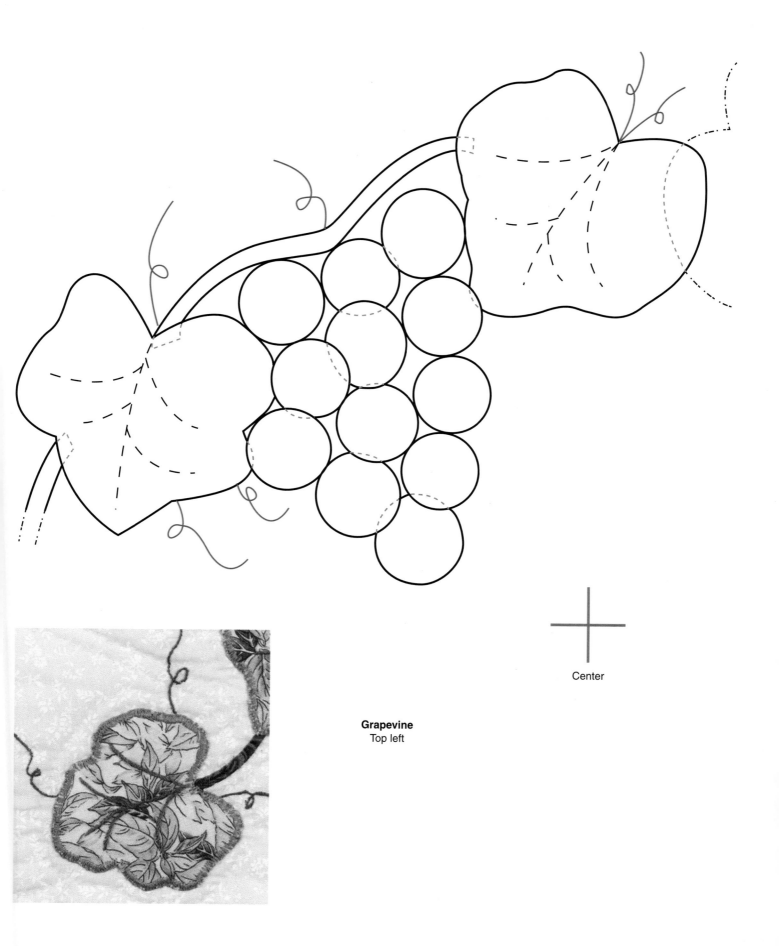

Center

Grapevine
Top left

Vine of Sodom

For their vine is of the vine of Sodom, and of the fields of Gomorrah: their grapes are grapes of gall, their clusters are bitter:
—Deuteronomy 32:32

There are several references to the Sodom apple in books I have read. Some authors refer to it as the "Jericho potato." Some claim it is related to the eggplant. It is also known as "the Dead Sea vine" and "vine of Sodom." It is also called "Palestine nightshade."

In the Bible, thorns, briers and thistles tear at the soul. This bush is limited to the Dead Sea area and lower Jordan River.

The green unripe fruits, or apples, are eaten raw or added to soup.

The juice from the Sodom apple was used as a component in love potions.

When the fruit drops and is squeezed, it emits dust and ashes. These ashes may be the seeds. This is why the Sodom vine is also referred to as "dust and ashes." It grows in all hot valleys of the above locations.

Vine of Sodom
15" x 15" Block

Psalm 69:21 reads: "They gave me also gall for my meat; and in my thirst they gave me vinegar to drink." This could be a reference to the Sodom apple.

Project Specifications
Wall Quilt Size: 15" x 15"

Fabric & Batting
- Neutral background square 16 1/2" x 16 1/2"
- 1/4 yard red batik for appliqué and binding
- Scraps of white solid, 1 green print and 1 green batik for appliqué
- Backing 19" x 19"
- Batting 19" x 19"

Supplies & Tools
- Template material of choice
- Green and yellow 6-strand embroidery floss
- Appliqué thread of choice to match fabrics
- All-purpose thread to blend with fabrics
- 1 spool natural quilting thread

Instructions
1. Referring to photo for color suggestions, prepare templates and fabric for appliqué method of choice. Appliqué pieces on background square, except for three-dimensional flowers.

2. For gathered blossoms, trace three circles on white fabric using a quarter (25 cents) as a template. Leave at least 1/2" between circles. Place traced circles on a second piece of white fabric, right sides facing. Cut out the circles 1/4" outside the traced line

through both layers of fabric as shown in Figure 1. Repeat for three circle sets.

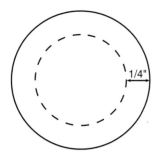

Figure 1
Cut circles 1/4" outside traced line.

3. Sew a running stitch on the traced line. Knot at both ends and do not gather the thread. Carefully cut a small X in the

center of one circle as shown in Figure 2. Turn the circles right side out through the slits and make five marks as shown in Figure 3. Repeat for all three circles.

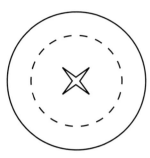

Figure 2
Cut a small X at the center of one layer of circle.

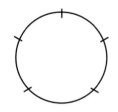

Figure 3
Turn circles right side out and mark 5 places as shown.

4. With knotted white sewing thread, come up through the center of the circle. Wrap the thread over the mark at the top of the circle and bring the needle up again at the center as shown in Figure 4. Pull the

thread up tight and knot, but do not cut. Repeat at each of the marks, working around the circle clockwise. This will create a five-petal flower (Figure 5).

Figure 4
Pull thread up tight and knot as shown.

Figure 5
5-petal flower.

5. With 3 strands of yellow 6-strand embroidery floss, make six French knots at the center of each blossom.

6. With 3 strands of green 6-strand embroidery floss, embroider veins on leaves with stem stitch as shown on pattern.

7. Trim background square to 15 1/2" x 15 1/2".

8. Layer backing, batting and block, and baste. Quilt as desired.

9. From red batik cut and piece 2 yards of 2 1/2"-wide strips for binding as shown in General Instructions. Bind to finish. ✳

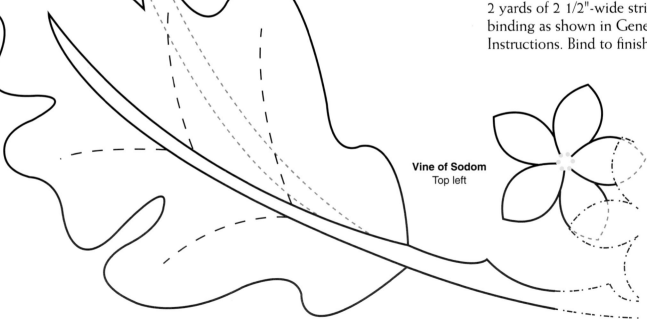

Vine of Sodom
Top left

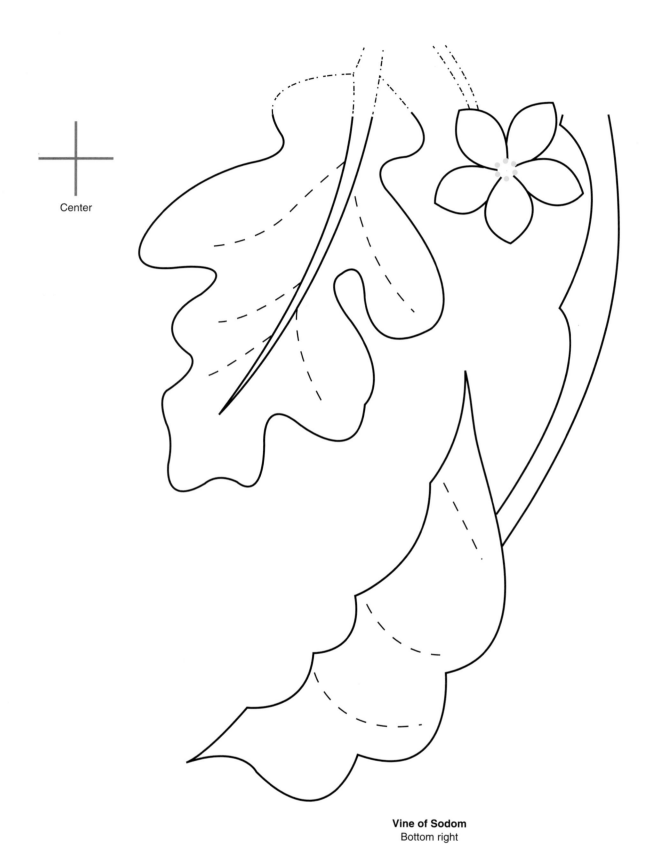

Center

Vine of Sodom
Bottom right

Vine of Sodom
Bottom left

Vine of Sodom
Top right

Henbane

The border went out unto the side of Ekron northward: and the border was drawn to Shicron, and passed along to mount Baalah, and went out unto Jabneel; and the goings out of the border were at the sea.

—Joshua 15:11

Henbane is a trailing plant growing wild around rocks and walls in the area described in the scripture passage above.

Project Specifications

Wall Quilt Size: 20 3/4" x 20 3/4"

Fabric & Batting

- Neutral background square 16 1/4" x 16 1/4"
- 1/4 yard purple-and-yellow print for center border
- 1/2 yard purple print for inner and outer borders and appliqué
- Scraps of green and brown print and pale lavender and yellow solid for appliqué
- 2 1/2 yards purchased or self-made lavender binding

Henbane
14 3/4" x 14 3/4" Block

- Backing 25" x 25"
- Batting 25" x 25"

Supplies & Tools

- Template material of choice
- Light gray and dark green 6-strand embroidery floss
- Appliqué thread of choice to match fabrics
- All-purpose thread to blend with fabrics
- Red, green and natural quilting threads

Instructions

1. Referring to photo for color suggestions, prepare templates and fabric for appliqué method of choice. Appliqué pieces on background square.

2. With 3 strands of light gray 6-strand embroidery floss, work a satin stitch over the stem areas between purple flower centers and pale lavender dangling appendages. With 3 strands of dark green 6-strand embroidery floss embroider stem-stitch veins on leaves as shown on pattern.

3. Trim background square to 15 1/4" x 15 1/4".

4. From purple print cut four strips each 1 3/8" x 22" and 1 1/4" x 22". From purple-and-yellow print cut four strips 1 7/8" x 22". Sew one purple-and-yellow print strip between a 1 3/8"-wide and a 1 1/4"-wide purple strip. Repeat for four borders. Press seams toward purple strips. Handle each piece as a single border and sew to center square, narrower purple strip next to the square, as in General Instructions. Miter corners. Trim to square.

5. Layer backing, batting and block, and baste. Quilt as desired.

6. Bind quilt to finish. ✳

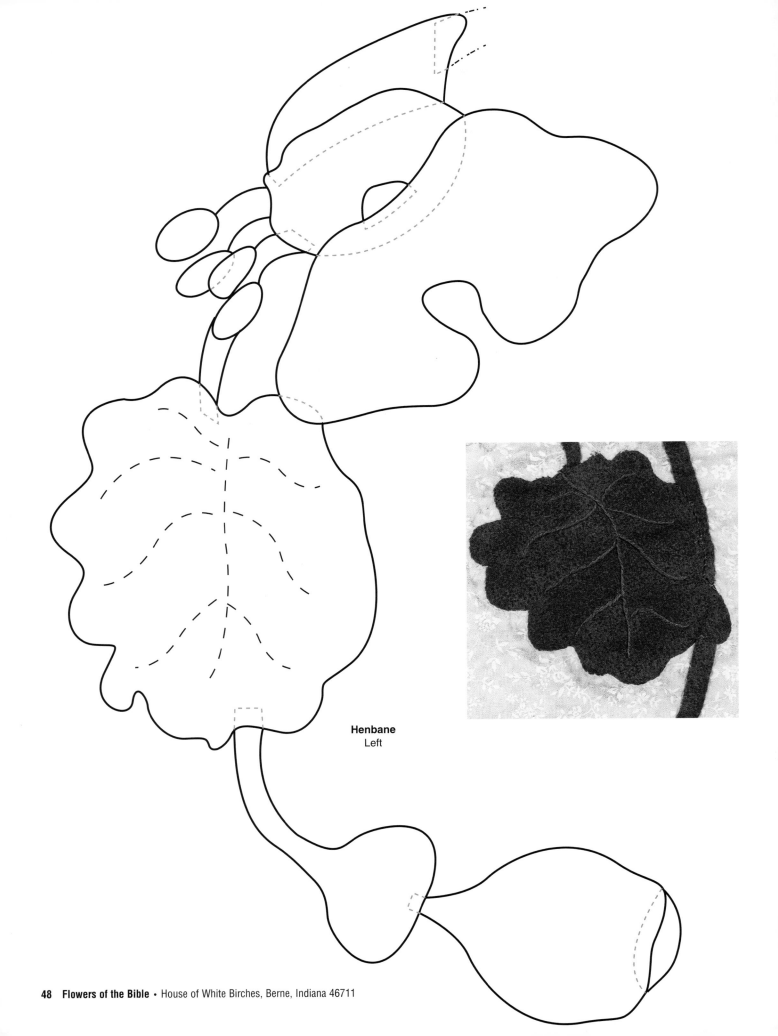

Henbane
Left

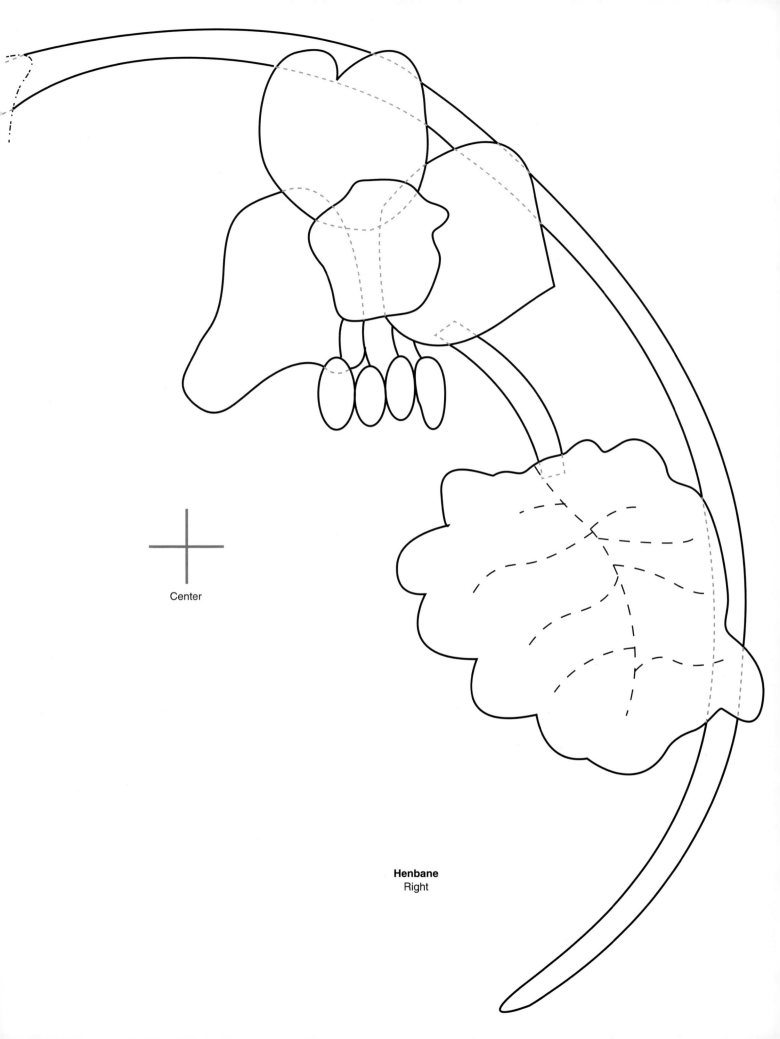

Center

Henbane
Right

Water Lily

And the chapiters that were upon the top of the pillars were of lily work in the porch, four cubits.
—I Kings 7:19
—Also I Kings 7:22–26

(In Egypt, the same pattern of lily designs is seen on the top of pillars.)

The water lily (lotus), at the time of King Solomon, was a rich blue with yellow anthers of clear yellow.

When King Solomon inherited the Kingdom from his father, David, and his mother, Bathsheba, a conniver, he went to Egypt to visit the current Pharaoh. Egypt was no special threat, so he cemented ties with that country and was offered a young girl to wed. She was a royal princess.

Today, with advanced archaeological finds, we have learned the water lily was used by Egyptians as Viagra is used today.

Solomon firmed up his friendship with Hiram, the ruler of the Phoenicians, who were first-class craftspeople. Hiram of Tyre directed his craftsmen

Water Lily
14 3/4" x 14 3/4" Block

to decorate the chapiters on top of the pillars with water lilies (lotus).

Since Solomon had the largest female hoard in history, 700 wives and 300 women concubines, he may have appreciated the lily such as the Egyptians had.

King Solomon was the King Ludwig of the Holy Lands. While Ludwig built castles, Solomon built temples. Because of his expanding family, Solomon had to spend 13 years increasing the size of his compound. The land of milk and honey, wells and brooks was partly destroyed by Solomon's building frenzy. He was one of the first recorded plunderers of the forests. Additional insult to the land was the goats permitted to graze the deforested slopes. This area has become one of the most impoverished areas in the world. It has never regained its original beauty.

Project Specifications
Wall Quilt Size: 17 1/4" x 17 1/4"

Fabric & Batting
- Neutral background square 16 1/4" x 16 1/4"
- 1/4 yard medium blue marbled fabric for center border and appliqué
- 1/2 yard medium green print for inner border, binding and appliqué
- Scraps of medium green print, yellow and gold solid for appliqué
- Backing 21" x 21"
- Batting 21" x 21"

Supplies & Tools
- Template material of choice
- Appliqué thread of choice to match fabrics
- All-purpose thread to blend with fabrics
- Gold 6-strand embroidery floss
- 1 spool natural quilting thread

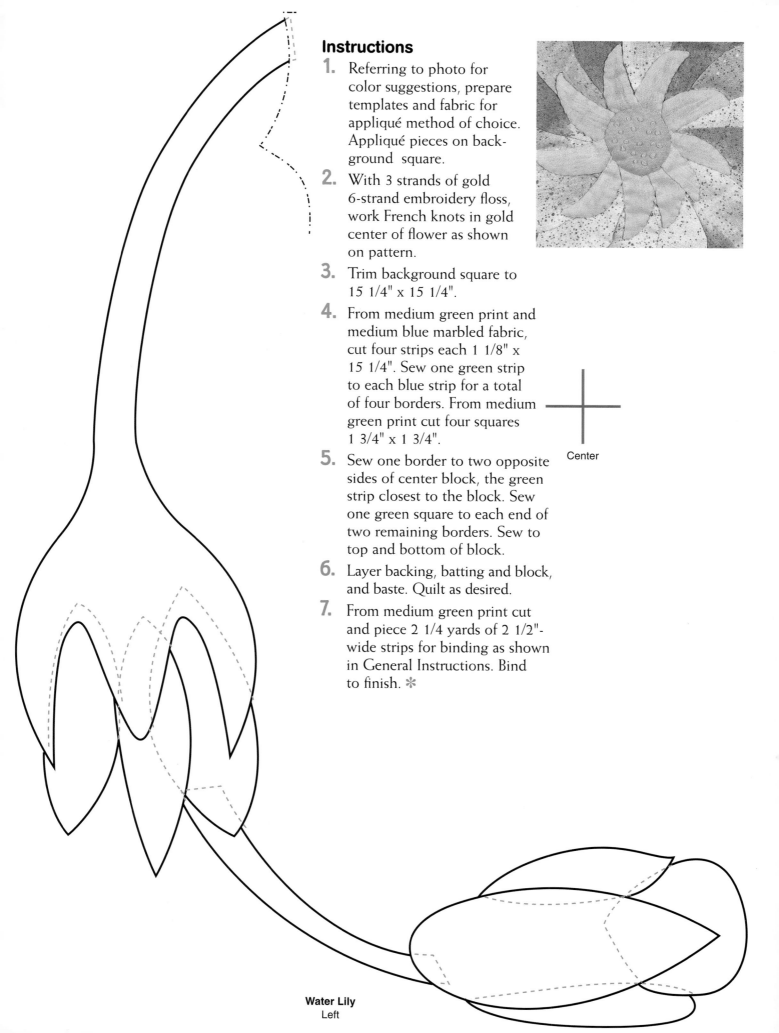

Instructions

1. Referring to photo for color suggestions, prepare templates and fabric for appliqué method of choice. Appliqué pieces on background square.

2. With 3 strands of gold 6-strand embroidery floss, work French knots in gold center of flower as shown on pattern.

3. Trim background square to 15 1/4" x 15 1/4".

4. From medium green print and medium blue marbled fabric, cut four strips each 1 1/8" x 15 1/4". Sew one green strip to each blue strip for a total of four borders. From medium green print cut four squares 1 3/4" x 1 3/4".

5. Sew one border to two opposite sides of center block, the green strip closest to the block. Sew one green square to each end of two remaining borders. Sew to top and bottom of block.

6. Layer backing, batting and block, and baste. Quilt as desired.

7. From medium green print cut and piece 2 1/4 yards of 2 1/2"-wide strips for binding as shown in General Instructions. Bind to finish. ✳

Center

Water Lily
Left

Water Lily

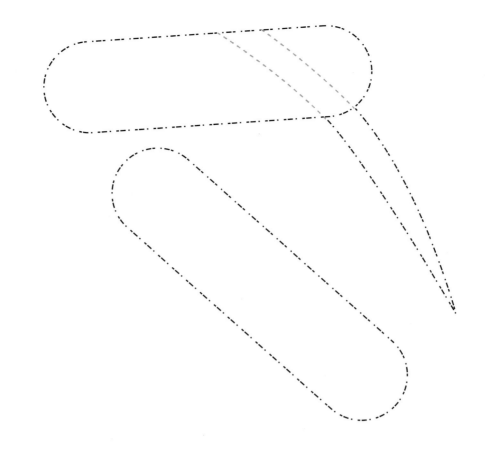

Cattails
Bottom

Mallow

Who cut up mallows by the bushes, and juniper roots for their meat.

—Job 30:4

The mallow was originally called "malluach," meaning saltiness, either taste or location.

The plant grew wild in the Holy Lands, particularly in the salty maritime regions. It is supposed that Job lived in Eastern Syria near the Euphrates River. Now it is thought that the land of Uz was much further south, east of the Sinai Peninsula.

Since the time of Job several species of mallow have occurred. It is therefore difficult to identify the original strain.

Mallow
14 1/2" X 14 1/2" Block

Project Specifications

Wall Quilt Size: 18" x 18"

Fabric & Batting

- Neutral background square 16" x 16"
- 1/4 yard teal batik for inner border
- 1/4 yard dark red print for center border and appliqué
- 1/4 yard green print for outer border
- Scraps of yellow, purple and green solid, and green, dark red and rose print for appliqué
- 2 1/4 yards purchased or self-made dark red binding
- Backing 22" x 22"
- Batting 22" x 22"

Supplies & Tools

- Template material of choice
- Green 6-strand embroidery floss
- Appliqué thread of choice to match fabrics
- All-purpose thread to blend with fabrics
- Red, green and natural quilting threads

Instructions

1. Referring to photo for color suggestions, prepare templates and fabric for appliqué method of choice. Appliqué pieces on background square.

2. With 3 strands of green 6-strand embroidery floss, embroider veins on leaves with stem stitch as shown on pattern.

3. Trim square to 15" x 15".

4. From teal batik cut four strips 1 1/4" x 22". From dark red print and green print cut four strips each 1" x 22". Sew one red print strip between a teal batik strip and a green print strip. Repeat for four borders. Press seams toward inner and outer borders. Handle each piece as a single border and sew to center square as in General Instructions, batik border nearest appliquéd block. Miter corners. Trim to square.

5. Layer backing, batting and block, and baste. Quilt as desired.

6. Bind quilt to finish. ✳

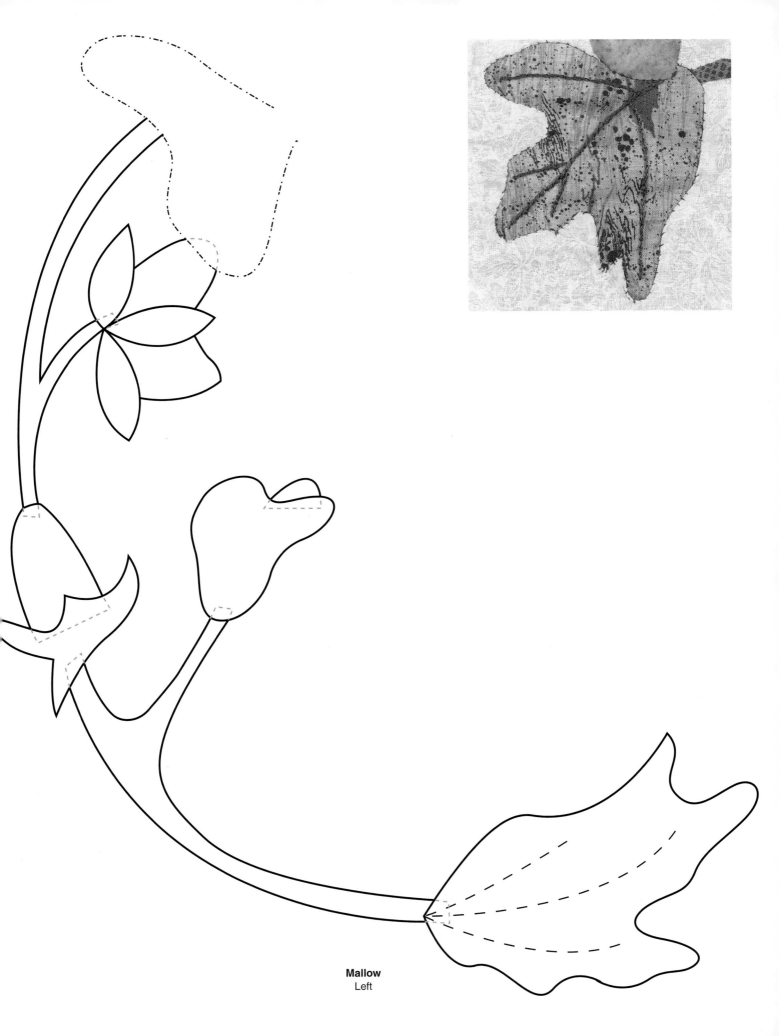

Mallow
Left

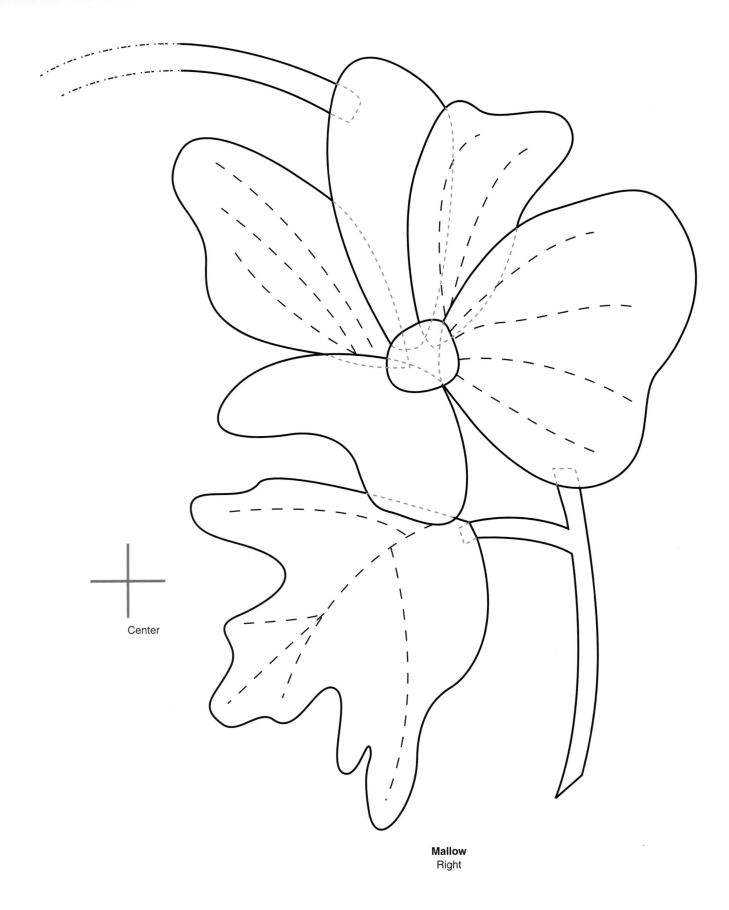

Center

Mallow
Right

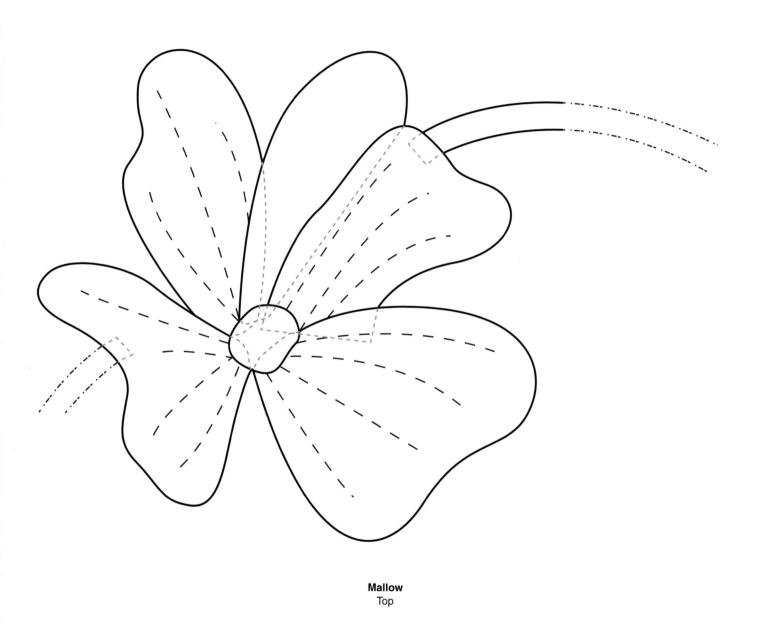

Mallow
Top

Cockle & Raven

Let thistles grow instead of wheat,
and cockle instead of barley.
The words of Job are ended.
—Job 31:40

The cockle is a pervasive plant, today known as a weed, that grew between edible plants. If the seeds of the cockle were ground together with the edible seed, discomfort or death could occur.

Who provideth for the raven his food?
When his young ones cry unto God,
they wander for lack of meat.

—Job 38:41

Behold the fowls of the air: for they sow not, neither do they reap, nor gather into barns; yet your heavenly Father feedeth them. Are ye not much better than they?

—Matthew 6:26

Basically, the raven is a scavenger. It has an ominous connotation. Edgar Allan Poe made use of its meaning. It will feast on carrion.

Cockle
15" x 15" Block

Project Specifications
Wall Quilt Size: 24" x 24"

Fabric & Batting
• Neutral background square

16 1/2" x 16 1/2"
• 1/4 yard pink solid for center border and appliqué
• 5/8 yard green leaf print for inner and outer borders
• Scraps of black, white, green and yellow solid, 3 shades of pink solid, and gray and green prints for appliqué
• 3 yards purchased or self-made dark green binding
• Backing 28" x 28"
• Batting 28" x 28"

Supplies & Tools
• Template material of choice
• 1 dark red seed bead for raven eye
• Black and yellow 6-strand embroidery floss
• Appliqué thread of choice to match fabrics
• All-purpose thread to blend with fabrics
• 1 spool natural quilting thread

Instructions
1. Referring to photo for color suggestions, prepare templates and fabric for appliqué method of choice. Appliqué pieces on background square.

2. With 3 strands of black 6-strand embroidery floss, embroider details on flowers as shown on pattern. With 3 strands of yellow 6-strand embroidery floss, add French knots to yellow flower centers.

3. Trim background square to 15 1/2" x 15 1/2".

4. From green leaf print cut eight strips 2 1/4" x 28". From pink solid fabric cut four strips

1 1/2" x 28". Sew one pink strip between two green leaf print strips. Repeat for four borders. Press seams away from pink strips. Handle each piece as a single border and sew to center square as in General Instructions. Miter corners. Trim to square.

5. Referring to photo for placement, arrange raven on lower right corner. Appliqué pieces on background. Place small white scrap behind eye area and reverse-appliqué eye. Sew dark red seed bead in center of eye.

6. Layer backing, batting and block, and baste. Quilt as desired. Quilt detail lines on raven as shown on pattern.

7. Bind quilt to finish. ✳

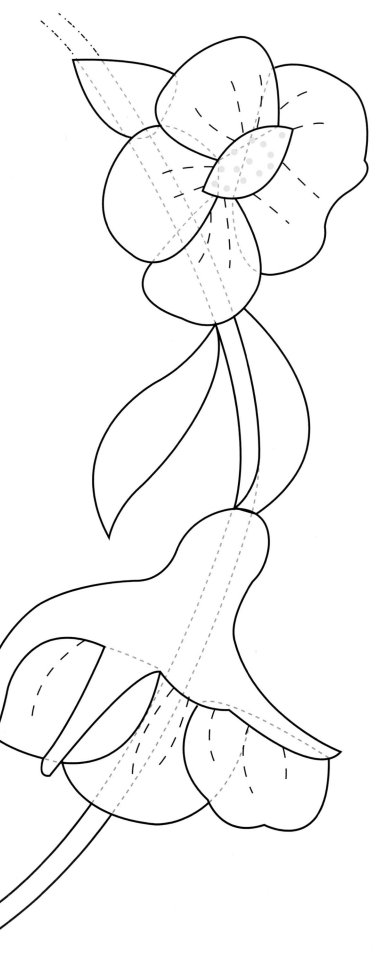

Cockle
Right

Raven Placement Diagram

Center

Cockle
Left

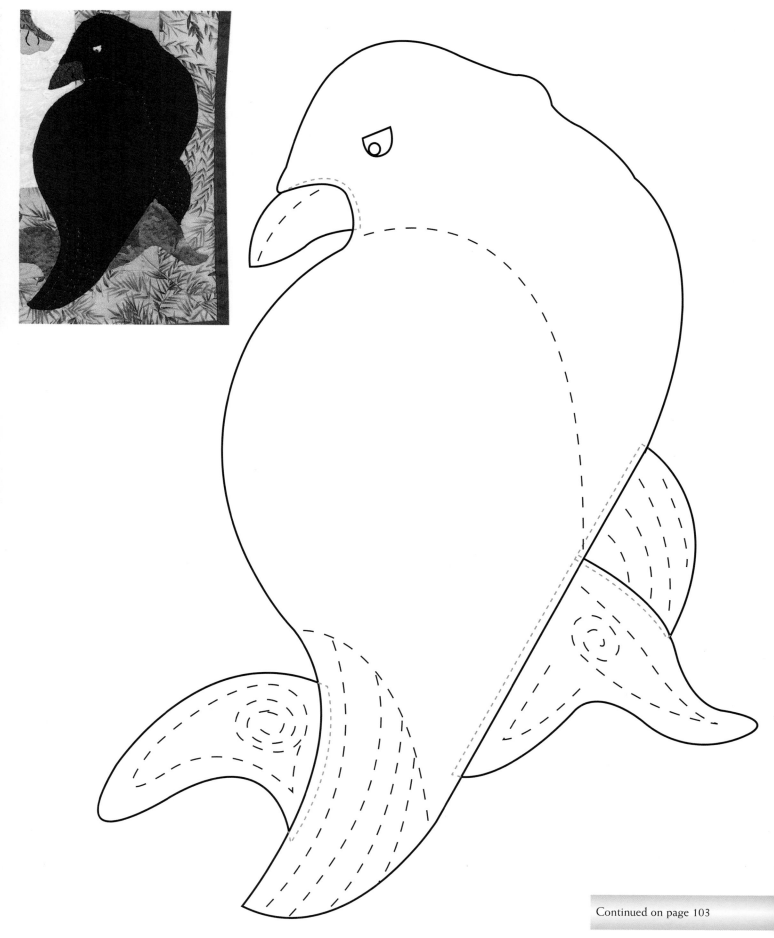

Raven

Continued on page 103

Caper Bush

Also when they shall be afraid of that which is high, and fears shall be in the way, and the almond tree shall flourish, and the grasshopper shall be a burden, and desire shall fail: because man goeth to his long home, and the mourners go about the streets.
—Ecclesiastes 12:5

When in Ecclesiastes it states "desire shall fail," the ancient Israelites served capers as an appetizer, which was to abate hunger until the main course was ready to eat.

The caper bush grows everywhere in Palestine, Syria and Lebanon. Heavy draping branches cover walls of Jerusalem and rocks of many valleys. Large white flowers bloom one night. In ancient times caper berries were also used to stimulate sexual desire.

It is also believed capers could be beneficial for arthritis, cancer, cataracts, dysentery, fractures, malaria and sciatica. What was left for a doctor to heal?

Caper Bush
14 1/2" x 14 1/2" Block

An accompanying verb "tapher" is translated either to fail or burst, thus illustrating the failing powers of an old man, loss of taste and appetite. The Spanish believe eating capers holds off old age.

Project Specifications
Wall Quilt Size: 18" x 18"

Fabric & Batting
- Neutral background square 16" x 16"
- 1/4 yard lavender print for center border and binding
- 1/4 yard purple solid for outer border
- 1/8 yard lavender solid for inner border and appliqué
- Pale lavender print and green print and solid scraps for appliqué
- Backing 22" x 22"
- Batting 22" x 22"

Supplies & Tools
- Template material of choice
- Light green and purple 6-strand embroidery floss
- Appliqué thread of choice to match fabrics
- All-purpose thread to blend with fabrics
- 1 spool natural quilting thread

Instructions
1. Referring to photo for color suggestions, prepare templates and fabric for appliqué method of choice. Appliqué pieces on background square.

Center

Caper Bush
Left

2. With 3 strands of purple 6-strand embroidery floss, work satin stitch over flower stamens, and stem-stitch detail as shown on pattern. Work stem stitch around outside edge of flowers.

3. With 3 strands of light green 6-strand embroidery floss, embroider leaf veins with stem stitch.

4. Trim background square to 15" x 15".

5. From lavender solid cut four strips 1" x 22". From lavender print cut four strips 1" x 22". From purple solid cut four strips 1 1/4" x 22". Sew one lavender print strip between a lavender solid strip and a purple solid strip. Repeat for four borders. Press seams toward lavender print and purple borders. Handle each piece as a single border and sew to center square as in General Instructions, solid lavender border nearest appliquéd block. Miter corners. Trim to square.

6. Layer backing, batting and block, and baste. Quilt as desired.

7. From lavender print cut and piece 2 1/4 yards of 2 1/2"-wide strips for binding as shown in General Instructions. Bind to finish. ✳

Caper Bush
Right

Caper Bush
Top

Tulip

I am the rose of Sharon, and the lily of the valleys.
—Song of Solomon 2:1

Because so many of us have a Rose of Sharon growing in our gardens, I get one request after another to design a Rose of Sharon biblical block.

Sadly, there is no such biblical flower. The flower that grew in the Plain of Sharon, about 60 miles long between Carmel and Jaffa, was a red tulip, a native plant of the Holy Lands. Although it was referred to as a rose in Song of Solomon, it grew from a bulb and was about 10 inches tall. Therefore, we know it was not a rose.

In 1634, a tulip mania gripped the land. Fantastic prices were paid for new strains, with a single bulb bringing in as much as $1,725. Some investors lost everything gambling on the tulip market.

Tulip
14 1/2" x 14 1/2" Block

Project Specifications
Wall Quilt Size: 21 1/2" x 21 1/2"

Fabric & Batting
- Neutral background square 16" x 16"

- 1/4 yard lime green solid for outer border and appliqué
- 1/4 yard dark red solid for inner border and appliqué
- 1/4 yard medium red solid for center border and appliqué
- Scraps of dark green solid and red print for appliqué
- 2 5/8 yards purchased or self-made dark green binding
- Backing 25" x 25"
- Batting 25" x 25"

Supplies & Tools
- Template material of choice
- Appliqué thread of choice to match fabrics
- All-purpose thread to blend with fabrics
- Red, green and natural quilting threads

Instructions
1. Referring to photo for color suggestions, prepare templates and fabric for appliqué method of choice. Appliqué pieces on background square. Trim background square to 15" x 15".

2. From lime green solid cut four strips 2" x 22". From medium red solid cut four strips 1 1/2" x 22". From dark red solid cut four strips 1 1/2" x 22". Sew one medium red strip between a dark red strip and a lime green strip. Repeat for four borders. Press seams toward medium red and green borders. Handle each piece as a single border and sew to center square as in General Instructions, dark red border nearest appliquéd block. Miter corners. Trim to square.

3. Layer backing, batting and block, and baste. Quilt as desired.

4. Bind quilt to finish. ✳

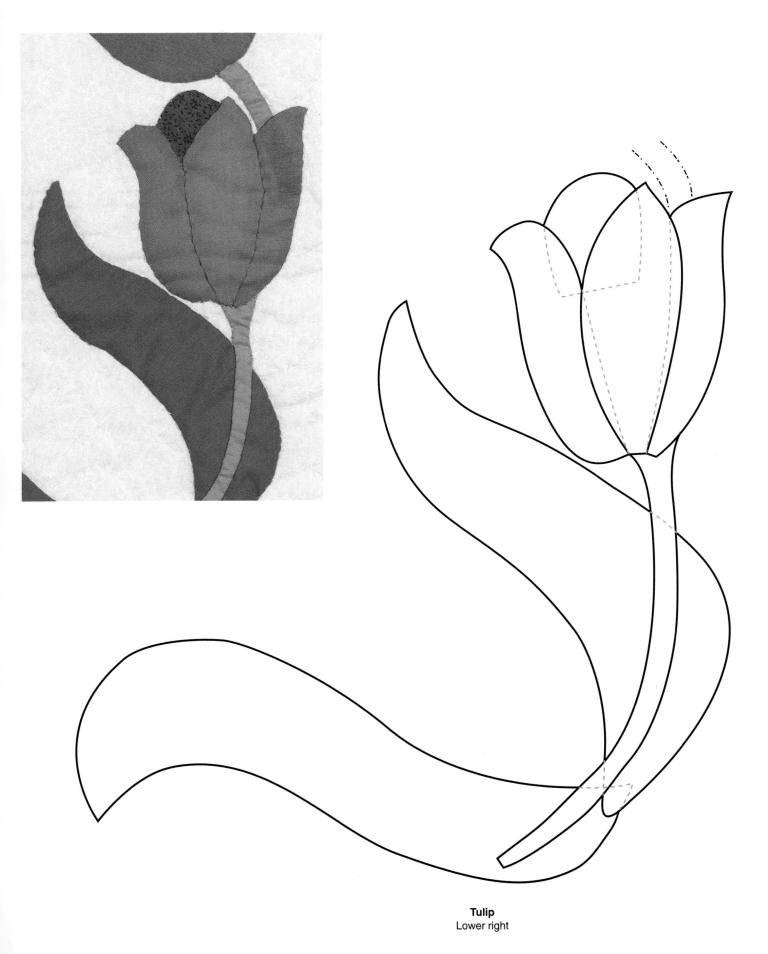

Tulip
Lower right

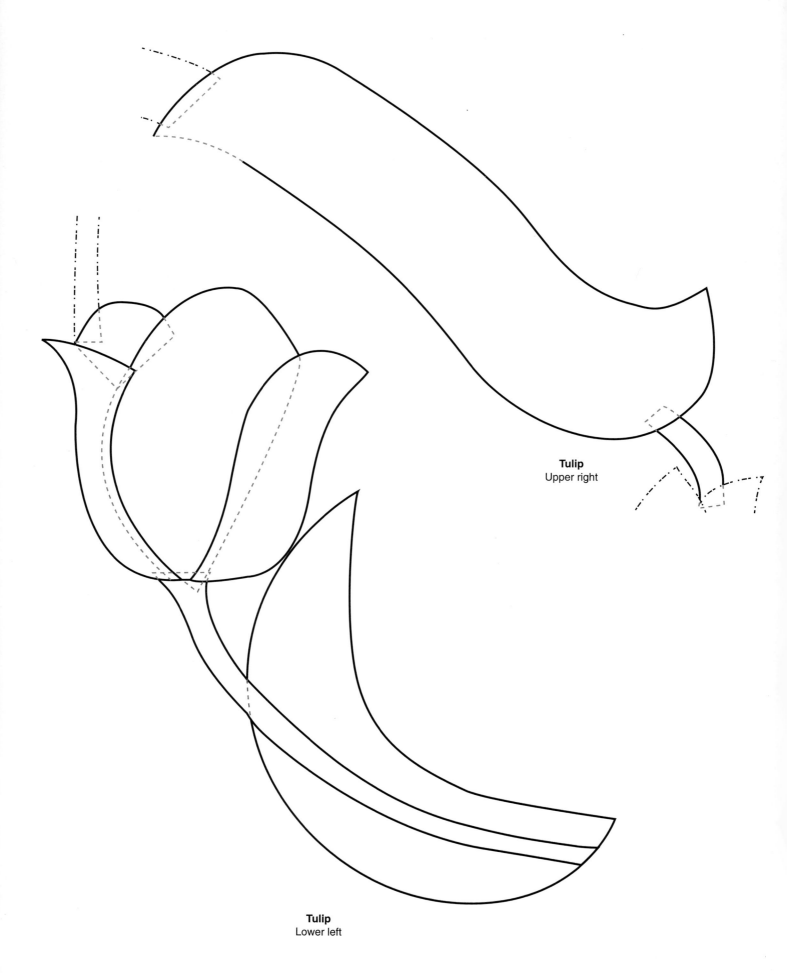

Tulip
Upper right

Tulip
Lower left

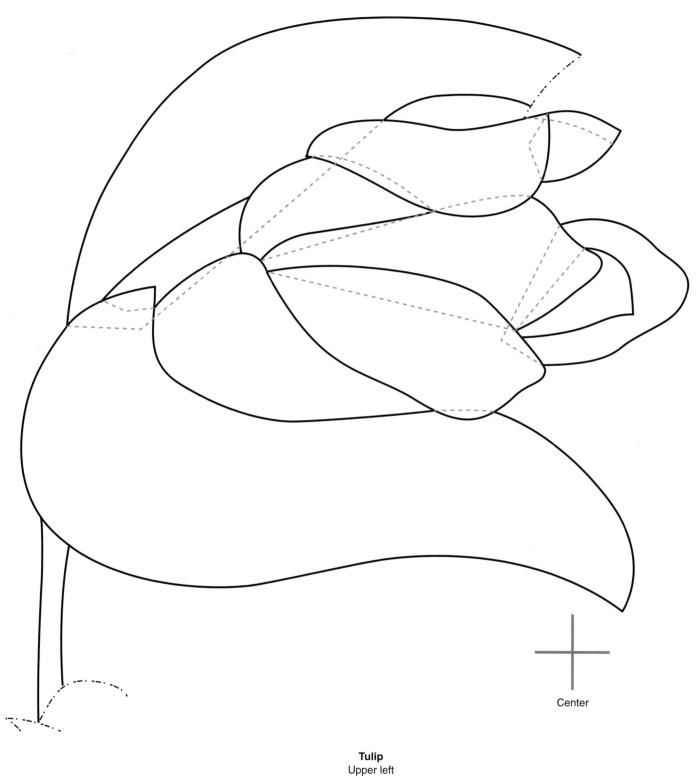

Center

Tulip
Upper left

Pomegranate

According to Jewish legend, there are 613 seeds in the pomegranate, the same number of laws God gave to Israel.

Ancient legends proclaim the pomegranate as the "Tree of Life" in the Garden of Eden. It was a symbol of hope of eternal life.

Ceres, goddess of earth, became enraged when Zeus gave her daughter to Pluto, the god of the underworld, as his wife. Ceres left Heaven in her rage and came down to earth, blessing all men who were kind to her and cursing all who were unkind. She cursed so many men that Zeus saw his mistake and demanded Pluto give up Proserpine. This he did, but first asked his bride to eat a pomegranate. Doing so, she remained in his power and he had her return to Hades six months of the year. Ceres was happy to have her daughter back as company. The earth was again green and fruitful. When Ceres was lonely and angry, the earth was cold, bare and barren. Because of this story the Greeks and Romans associated the pomegranate with the netherworld and believed all seeds had to be planted in the soil underground to germinate.

The pomegranate is a most healthy fruit. It contains potassium and vitamin C; is high in vitamin B, copper and estrogen; and has only 105 calories per fruit.

Pomegranate syrup is known as grenadine, and leather dyed from the fruit is cordovan. It has better heart protection than red wine. Japanese studies show that the fruit can ease symptoms of menopause.

Pomegranate
14 3/4" x 14 3/4" Block

Project Specifications
Wall Quilt Size: 19 1/4" x 19 1/4"

Fabric & Batting
- Neutral background square 16 1/4" x 16 1/4"
- 1/4 yard red mottled print for center border and appliqué
- 3/8 yard medium green print for inner and outer borders and appliqué
- Scraps of green, gold and red solid, red and light and dark green print for appliqué
- 2 1/3 yards purchased or self-made dark green binding
- Backing 23" x 23"
- Batting 23" x 23"

Supplies & Tools
- Template material of choice

- Appliqué thread of choice to match fabrics
- All-purpose thread to blend with fabrics
- Gold 6-strand embroidery floss
- 1 spool natural quilting thread

Instructions

1. Referring to photo for color suggestions, prepare templates and fabric for appliqué method of choice. Appliqué pieces on background square. Trim background to 15 1/4" x 15 1/4".

2. With 3 strands of gold 6-strand embroidery floss, work French knots around gold centers of flowers as shown on pattern.

3. From medium green print cut eight strips 1 1/4" x 22". From red mottled print cut four strips 1 1/4" x 22". Sew one red strip between two green strips. Repeat for four borders. Press seams toward green borders. Handle each piece as a single border and sew to center square as in General Instructions. Miter corners. Trim to square.

4. Layer backing, batting and block, and baste. Quilt as desired.

5. Bind quilt to finish. ✳

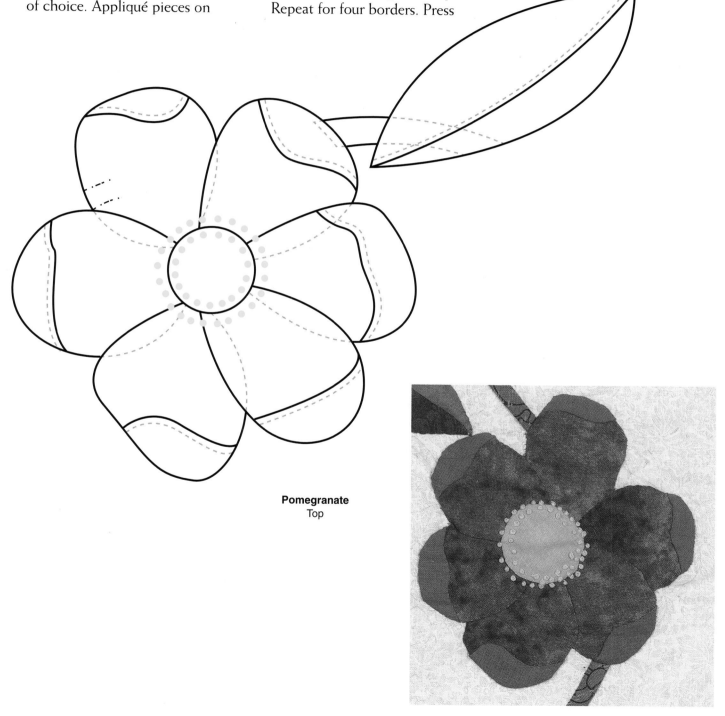

Pomegranate
Top

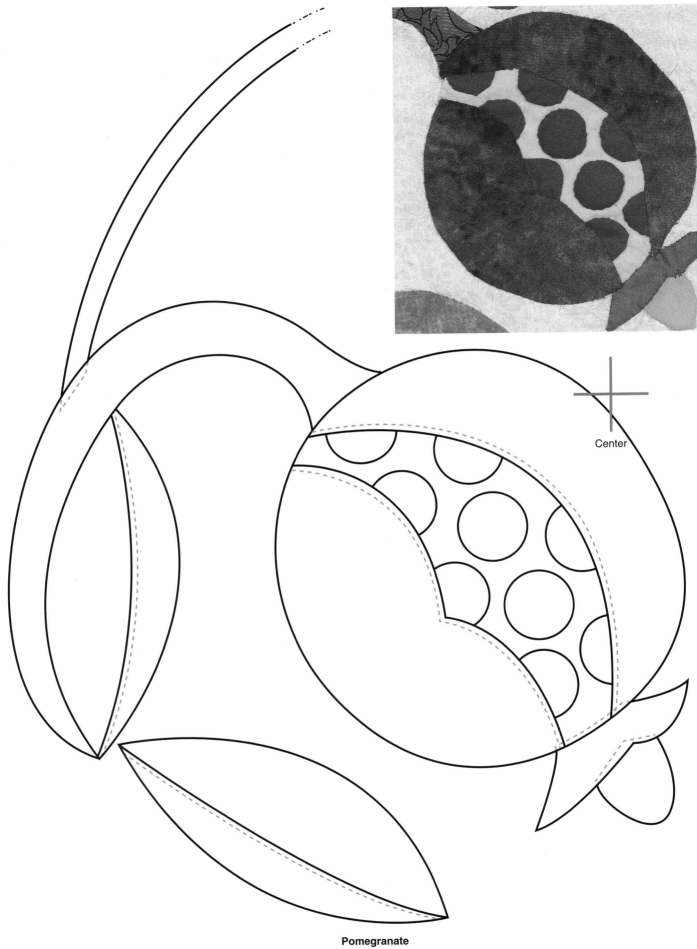

Center

Pomegranate
Left

Pomegranate
Right

Saffron Crocus

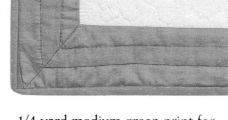

Spikenard and saffron; calamus and cinnamon, with all trees of frankincense; myrrh and aloes, with all the chief spices:
—Song of Solomon 4:14

The crocus we grow in our gardens today are slightly different from the ones in King Solomon's plot.

Many Jews in the saffron business had yellow hands and clothing, a result of weighing out the spice. Throughout the ages the color yellow has been used to mock the Jews. Nazi Germany forced Jews to wear a yellow Star of David on their clothing to distinguish them from Aryans.

Saffron is the most expensive spice in the world, taking 4,300 flowers to produce one ounce.

Overdoses of saffron are narcotic. Ten grams can be a lethal dose.

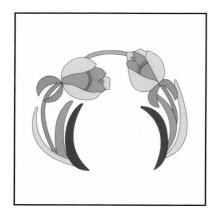

Saffron Crocus
15" x 15" Block

Project Specifications

Wall Quilt Size: 20 1/4" x 20 1/4"

Fabric & Batting

- Neutral background square 16 1/2" x 16 1/2"

- 1/4 yard medium green print for center border and appliqué
- 1/2 yard medium green solid for inner and outer borders and appliqué
- Scraps of dark green solid and dark green print and 4 shades of blue print for appliqué
- 2 1/2 yards purchased or self-made medium green binding
- Backing 24" x 24"
- Batting 24" x 24"

Supplies & Tools

- Template material of choice
- Appliqué thread of choice to match fabrics
- All-purpose thread to blend with fabrics
- Gold 6-strand embroidery floss
- 1 spool natural quilting thread

Instructions

1. Referring to photo for color suggestions, prepare templates and fabric for appliqué method of choice. Appliqué pieces on background square. Trim background square to 15 1/2" x 15 1/2".

2. With 3 strands of gold 6-strand embroidery floss, work French knots along the dark flower centers as shown on pattern. Embroider stem-stitch stamens and more French knots at their tips.

3. From medium green solid cut eight strips 1 3/8" x 22". From medium green print cut four strips 1 3/8" x 22". Sew one medium green print strip between two medium green solid strips. Repeat for four borders. Press seams toward center strip.

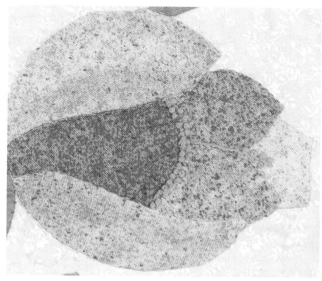

Handle each piece as a single border and sew to center square as in General Instructions. Miter corners. Trim to square.

4. Layer backing, batting and block, and baste. Quilt as desired.

5. Bind quilt to finish. *

Saffron Crocus
Right

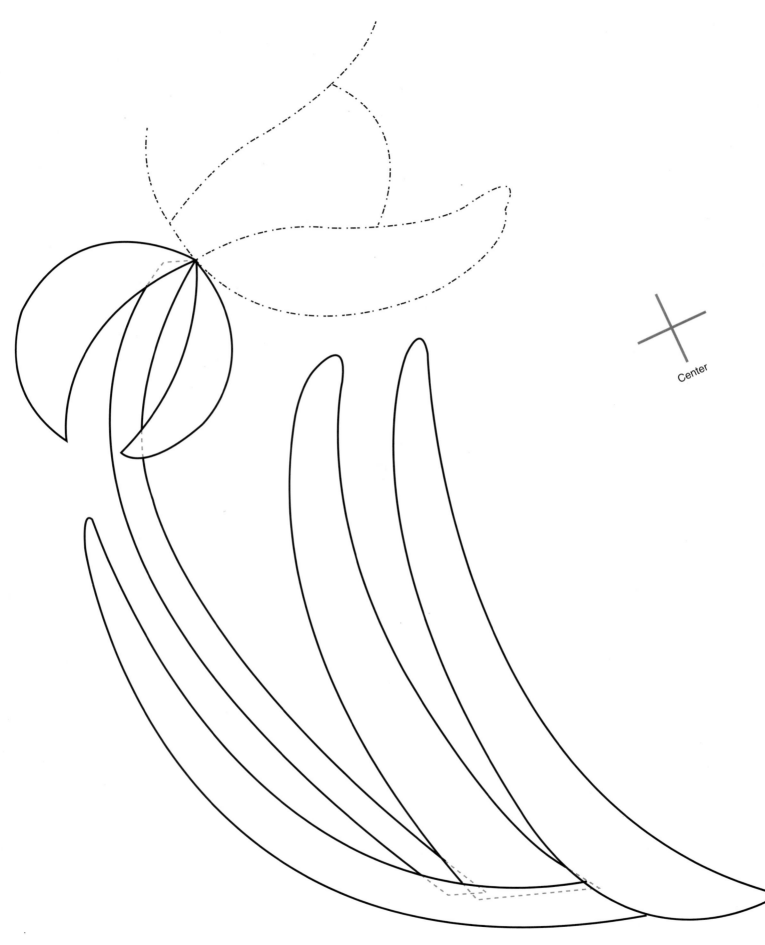

Center

Saffron Crocus
Left

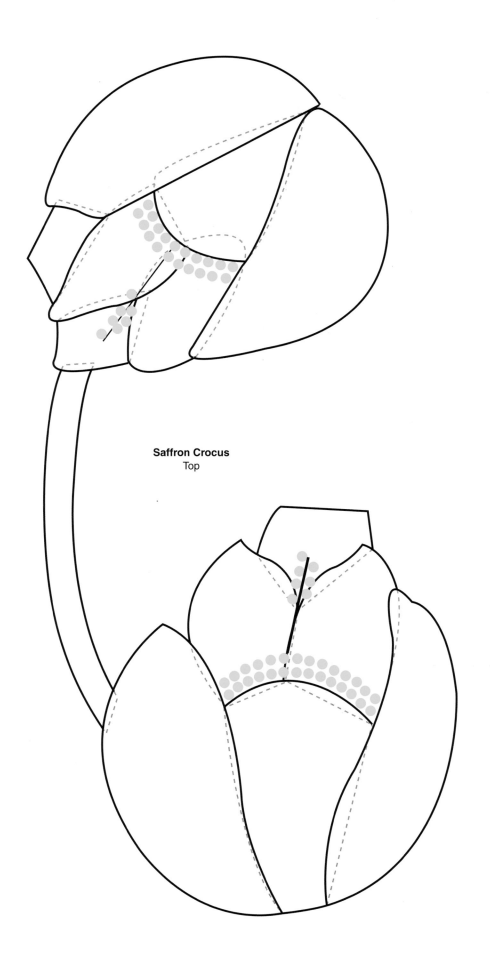

Saffron Crocus
Top

Turk's Cap Lily

His cheeks are as a bed of spices, as sweet flowers: his lips like lilies, dropping sweet smelling myrrh.
—Song of Solomon 5:13

The Turk's Cap Lily is a symbol of loveliness. There is an ancient legend that states all lilies were white and had erect flowers before they experienced the agony of Jesus in the Garden of Gethsemane. There, while all the other flowers drooped their heads in sympathetic grief over his suffering, the white lily, in her conceit at having been officially proclaimed more beautiful than Solomon's royal robes, proudly held her head up for him to admire. But, when Jesus' eyes fell upon the lily, the unspoken rebuke in his glance caused the haughty lily to contrast her conceit with his humility, and she blushed in shame. The red flush that tinged her face then is still evident today. Lilies still droop in shame of their former arrogance.

Some believe that the flower mentioned above was the anemone, but others insist it was the Turk's Cap Lily.

Turk's Cap Lily
15" x 14" Block

Project Specifications

Wall Quilt Size: 20" x 19"

Fabric & Batting

- Neutral background square 16 1/2" x 16 1/2"
- 1/4 yard rust print for inner border and appliqué
- 1/4 yard tan print for center border and appliqué
- 1/4 yard light green solid for outer border and appliqué
- Scraps of purple, pink, magenta, lavender and yellow solid; and teal, green and rust-and-brown print for appliqué
- 2 1/3 yards purchased or self-made brown binding
- Backing 24" x 23"
- Batting 24" x 23"

Supplies & Tools

- Template material of choice
- Appliqué thread of choice to match fabrics
- All-purpose thread to blend with fabrics
- 1 spool natural quilting thread

Instructions

1. Referring to photo for color suggestions, prepare templates and fabric for appliqué method of choice. Appliqué pieces on background square. Trim background to 15 1/2" x 14 1/2".

2. From rust print cut four strips 1 1/2" x 22". From tan print cut four strips 1 1/4" x 22". From light green solid cut four strips 1 1/4" x 22". Sew one tan print strip between a rust print strip and a light green solid strip. Repeat for four borders. Press seams toward tan borders. Handle each piece as a single

border and sew to cen-
ter square as in General
Instructions. Miter cor-
ners. Trim to square.

3. Layer backing, batting
and block, and baste.
Quilt as desired.

4. Bind quilt to finish. ✳

Center

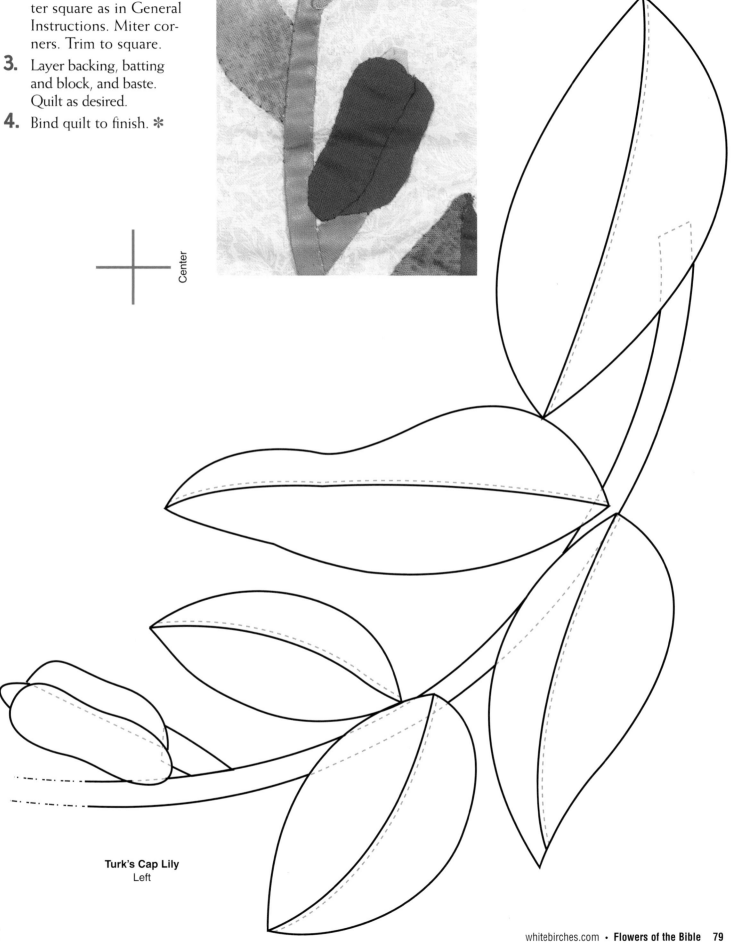

Turk's Cap Lily
Left

Turk's Cap Lily
Right

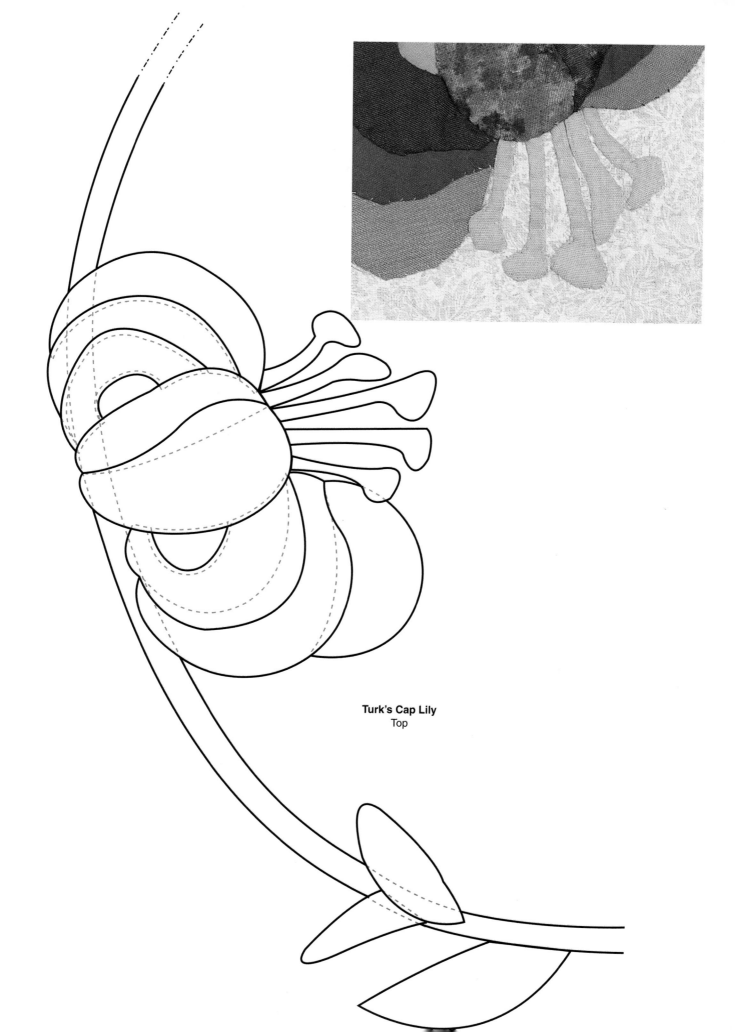

Turk's Cap Lily
Top

Narcissus

The wilderness and the solitary place shall be glad for them; and the desert shall rejoice, and blossom as the rose.
—Isaiah 35:1

The narcissus is believed to be the original lily. It grows abundantly in the plain of Sharon, on the hills at Jerusalem, Jericho and Mount Ebal and Sidom.

In Isaiah it relates the desert will rejoice and blossom like the rose. The narcissus is another flower wrongly named. A rose does not grow from a bulb, but does produce fruit called hips, which may have confused a non-botanical translator.

There is a Greek legend that tells about Narcissus, who failed to return the love of the nymph Echo, the daughter of Earth and Air, and how she pined away, leaving nothing but her voice. The handsome Narcissus was drowned when admiring his reflection in the water. A white narcissus sprang up at the spot where his body floated to shore.

This flower is a native of Israel.

Narcissus
15" x 15" Block

Project Specifications
Wall Quilt Size: 20" x 20"

Fabric & Batting
- Neutral background square 16 1/2" x 16 1/2"
- 1/4 yard medium green print for center border and appliqué
- 3/8 yard light green print for inner and outer borders
- Green, white, light and dark gold for appliqué
- 2 1/2 yards purchased or self-made light green binding
- Backing 24" x 24"
- Batting 24" x 24"

Supplies & Tools
- Template material of choice
- Appliqué thread of choice to match fabrics
- All-purpose thread to blend with fabrics
- Green 6-strand embroidery floss
- Embroidery needle
- 1 spool natural quilting thread

Instructions
1. Referring to photo for color suggestions, prepare templates and fabric for appliqué method of choice. Appliqué pieces on background square, except those flower centers marked with R on pattern, which have been reverse appliquéd. See General Instructions for reverse appliqué directions, if desired.
2. With 3 strands of green 6-strand embroidery floss, outline the white narcissus petals with a stem stitch.
3. Trim background square to 15 1/2" x 15 1/2".
4. From light green print cut eight strips 1 1/2" x 22". From medium green print cut four

strips 1" x 22". Sew a medium green strip between two light green strips Press seams toward medium green strip. Repeat for four borders. Handle each as a single border and sew to center square as in General Instructions. Miter corners and trim to square.

5. Layer backing, batting and block, and baste. Quilt as desired.

6. Bind quilt to finish. ✳

Narcissus
Top

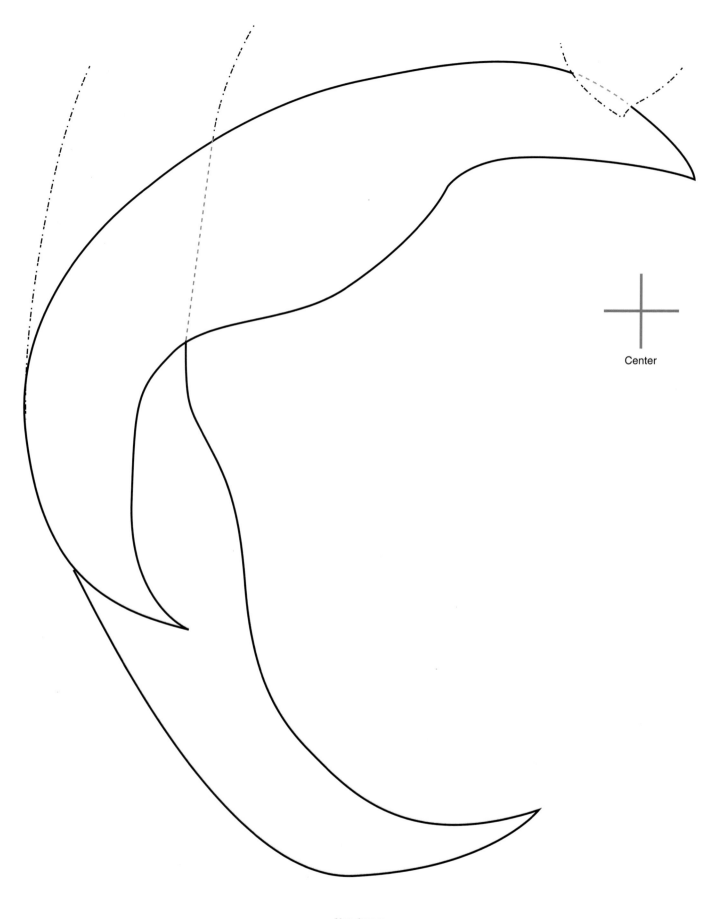

Narcissus
Left

Center

Narcissus
Right

Crown Anemone

In early spring it would seem the entire Mediterranean area is covered with anemones, also know as windflowers.

This is another wild flower referred to as "lily of the field." It was another plant, almost a weed, which grew between crops that had been planted for a purpose. It is abundant on Mount Olive as it was during the days of Jesus.

The Crown Anemone was a flower of ancient romance. The flower was to have sprung from the tears of Venus pining for Adonis. Where a tear dropped, a windflower grew.

Pliny declared that the flower only bloomed when the wind blew.

Crown Anemone
15" x 15" Block

Project Specifications
Wall Quilt Size: 18 3/4" x 18 3/4"

Fabric & Batting
- Neutral background square

16 1/2" x 16 1/2"
- 1/4 yard medium green print for center border and appliqué
- 3/8 yard red print for inner and outer borders and appliqué
- Red, pink and green scraps for appliqué
- 2 1/4 yards purchased or self-made medium green binding
- Backing 23" x 23"
- Batting 23" x 23"

Supplies & Tools
- Template material of choice
- Appliqué thread of choice to match fabrics
- All-purpose thread to blend with fabrics
- Black and green 6-strand embroidery floss
- Embroidery needle
- 1 spool natural quilting thread

Instructions
1. Referring to photo for color suggestions, prepare templates and fabric for appliqué method of choice. Appliqué pieces on background square.

2. Embroider leaf stems with stem stitch and 3 strands of green 6-strand embroidery floss. With 3 strands of black 6-strand embroidery floss, work French knots around the center of the anemones as shown on pattern.

3. Trim background square to 15 1/2" x 15 1/2".

4. From red print cut eight strips 1 1/8" x 22". From medium green print cut four strips 1 1/8" x 22". Sew a medium green strip between two red strips; press seams toward red strips. Repeat for four borders.

Handle each as a single border
and sew to center square as
in General Instructions. Miter
corners. Trim to square.

5. Layer backing, batting
and block, and baste. Quilt
as desired.

6. Bind quilt to finish. ✳

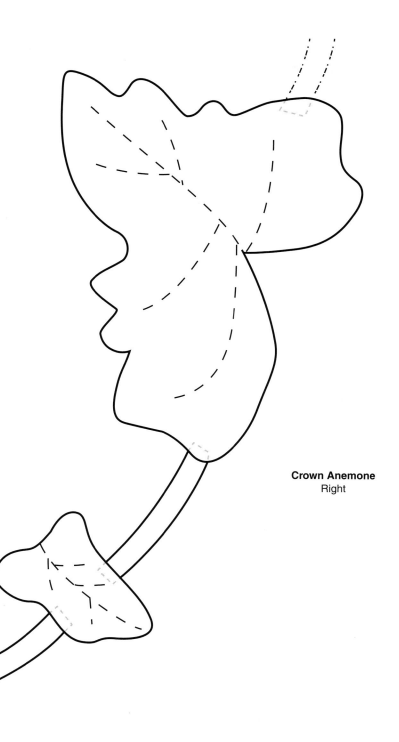

Crown Anemone
Right

Center

Crown Anemone
Left

Crown Anemone
Top

Common Poppy

The voice said, Cry. And he said, What shall I cry? All flesh is grass, and all the goodliness thereof is as the flower of the field.
—Isaiah 40:6

Jewish authorities recognized the danger of imbibing with opium more than 2,000 years ago. In the Talmud, the Jerushalmi warned against eating the "gall," as it was referred to.

Poppy seeds are used in baking and sprinkling on rolls and bread. It was believed that if you ingested these seeds you would have a suggestion of drugs in your urine analysis.

The poppy, which is a nuisance weed growing between the sown edible plants, was one that was referred to as lilies of the field.

We recognize poppies today as the flower sold by veterans as a fund-raiser. Soldiers fallen in trench warfare during World War I are remembered with poppies.

In Flanders fields the poppies blow
Between the crosses, row on row
That mark our place, and in the sky,
The larks, still bravely singing, fly.
—John McCrae

Common Poppy
15" x 15" Block

Project Specifications

Wall Quilt Size: 19 1/2" x 19 1/2"

Fabric & Batting

- Neutral background square 16 1/2" x 16 1/2"
- 1/4 yard dark green print for two borders and appliqué
- 1/4 yard medium green print for one border and appliqué
- 1/4 yard red print for one border, appliqué and binding.
- Scraps of green, cream and red for appliqué
- Backing 23" x 23"
- Batting 23" x 23"

Supplies & Tools

- Template material of choice
- Appliqué thread of choice to match fabrics
- All-purpose thread to blend with fabrics
- Black and red 6-strand embroidery floss
- Embroidery needle
- 1 spool natural quilting thread

Instructions

1. Referring to photo for color suggestions, prepare templates and fabric for appliqué method of choice. Appliqué pieces on the background square. Because of their small size, it might be easier to reverse-appliqué the leaves as shown on page 91. See General Instructions for reverse appliqué directions, if desired.

2. With 3 strands of black 6-strand embroidery floss, work satin

stitch over circles in center of poppy. With 2 strands of red 6-strand embroidery floss, work running stitch on lines marked on flower petals.

3. Trim background square to 15 1/2" x 15 1/2".

4. From dark green print cut four strips each 1 1/8" x 22" and 1" x 22". From medium green print cut four strips 1" x 22". From red solid cut four strips 1 1/8" x 22".

5. Sew together one 1"-wide dark green strip and one 1"-wide medium green strip. Sew one red solid strip to medium green strip and 1 1/8"-wide dark green strip to red. Repeat for four borders; press.

6. Sew a border to each side of center square, wider dark green strip closest to center block. Miter corners as in General Instructions and trim to square.

7. Layer backing, batting and block, and baste. Quilt as desired.

8. Bind quilt to finish. ✱

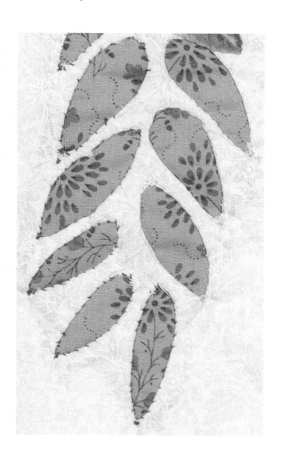

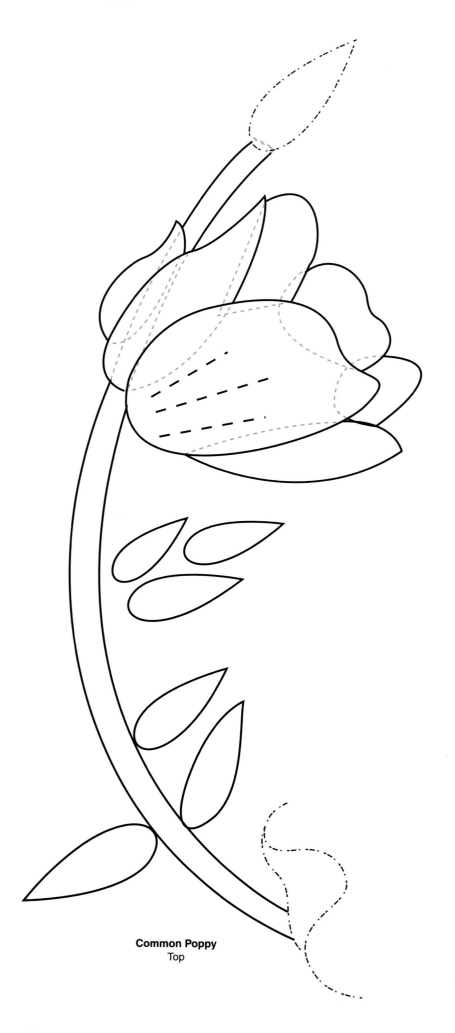

Common Poppy
Top

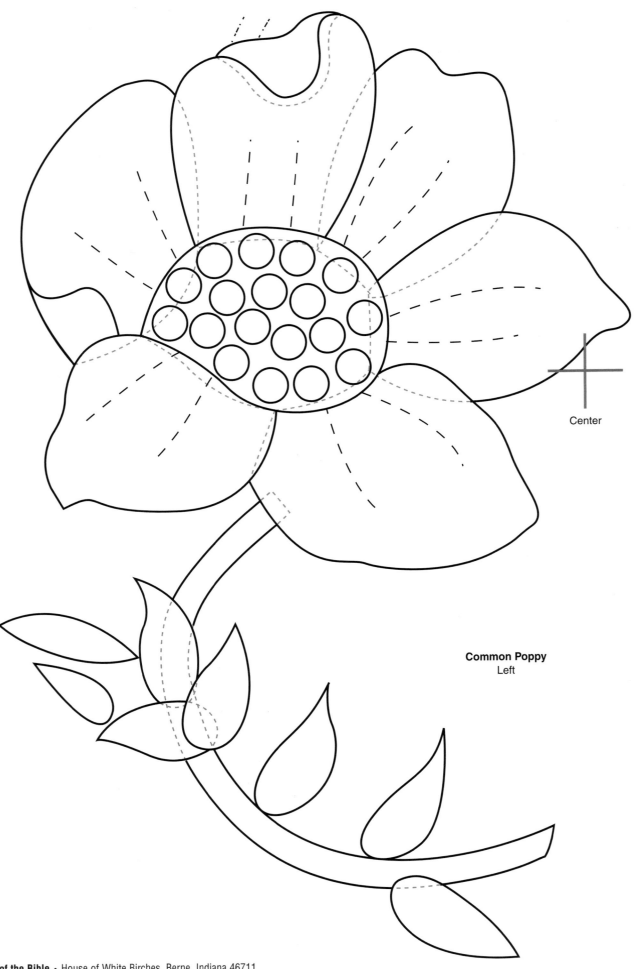

Center

Common Poppy
Left

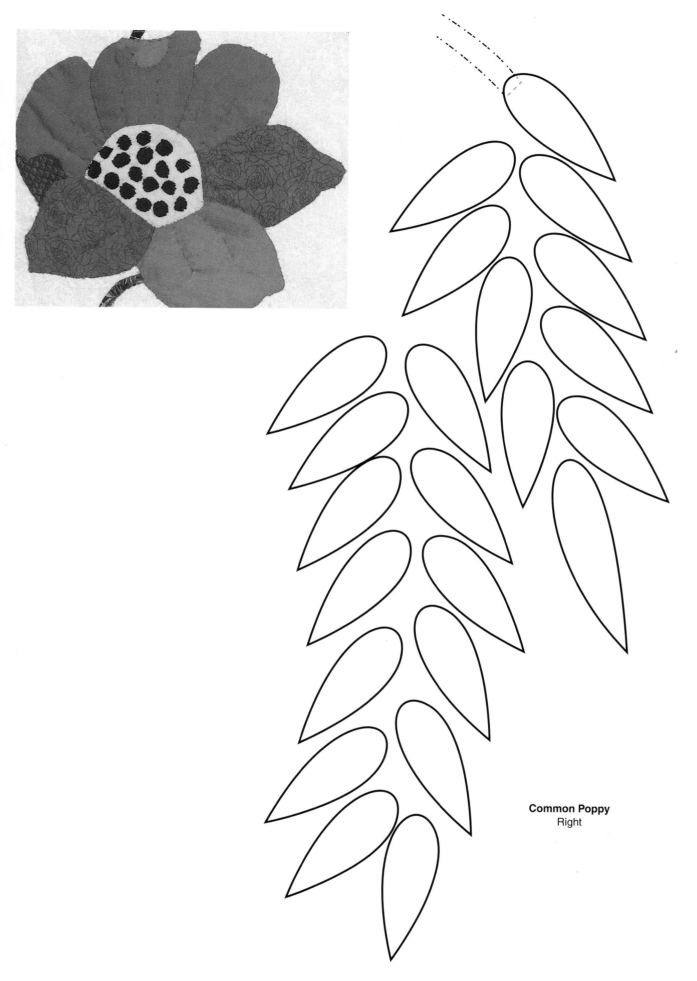

Common Poppy
Right

Common Myrtle

I will plant in the wilderness the cedar, the shittah tree, and the myrtle, and the oil tree; I will set in the desert the fir tree, and the pine, and the box tree together:
—Isaiah 41:19

Myrtle is a symbol of peace, divine blessing or divine generosity, and justice. Jews collect myrtle during the Feast of the Tabernacle, or Sukkoth.

Greeks considered myrtle as a symbol of love and immortality. They crowned their priest, heroes and outstanding men with myrtle. In Babylonia the myrtle tree designated the women who were brides. The Arabs believe that myrtle was one of the three plants taken out of the Garden of Eden.

Myrtle was sacred to Venus as a symbol of sensual love and passion.

There is a legend that Myrene was changed into a myrtle tree when she beat Minerva in a foot race. When Venus found her son Cupid had fallen in love with Psyche, she beat the nymph with a myrtle branch.

Myrtle
14" x 14" Block

Because of its sweet smell, the Jews referred to it as "hadas," meaning sweetness, hence: Hadassah, the name of a Jewish women's association.

Project Specifications
Wall Quilt Size: 17 3/4" x 17 3/4"

Fabric & Batting
- Neutral background square 15 1/2" x 15 1/2"
- 1/8 yard dark green print for center border
- 1/4 yard light blue print for inner and outer borders
- Light and dark blue, green, gold and tan scraps for appliqué
- 4 squares navy solid 2 3/8" x 2 3/8" for corner squares
- 2 1/4 yards purchased or self-made dark blue binding
- Backing 21" x 21"
- Batting 21" x 21"

Supplies & Tools
- Template material of choice
- Appliqué thread of choice to match fabrics
- All-purpose thread to blend with fabrics
- Green and white 6-strand embroidery floss
- Embroidery needle
- 1 spool natural quilting thread

Instructions
1. Referring to photo for color suggestions, prepare templates and fabric for appliqué method of choice. Appliqué pieces on background square.
2. From light blue scraps cut 10 circles 2 3/4" in diameter. Fold each circle in half and then in

quarters. Run a gathering thread 1/4" from curved edge of each as shown in Figure 1 to make petals. Pull up gathers and knot. Referring to pattern, arrange five petals each to make two flowers. Tack lightly in place. Appliqué gold flower centers in place to cover raw edges of petals.

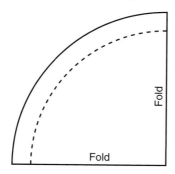

Figure 1
Run a gathering thread 1/4" from curved edge as shown.

3. With 3 strands of white 6-strand embroidery floss, work ten French knots in each flower center. With 2 strands of white embroidery floss, make long stitches from flower center to the end of each petal and from flower center to between petals. End each stitch with a French knot as shown in Figure 2.

Figure 2
Make long stitches ending in French knots placed as shown.

4. With 3 strands of green 6-stand embroidery floss, embroider stem stitch veins on leaves as shown on pattern.

5. Trim background square to 14 1/2" x 14 1/2".

6. From light blue print cut eight strips 1 1/8" x 14 1/2". From dark green print cut four strips 1 1/8" x 14 1/2". Sew a dark strip between two light blue strips. Press seams toward green strip. Repeat for four borders.

7. Sew a border strip to two opposite sides of center square. Sew a 2 3/8" x 2 3/8" navy solid square to each end of two remaining border strips. Sew to top and bottom of center square.

8. Layer backing, batting and block, and baste. Quilt as desired.

9. Bind quilt to finish. ✳

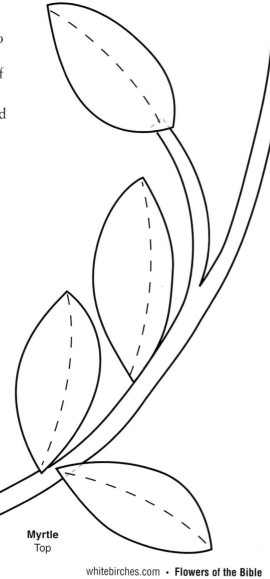

Myrtle
Top

Center

Myrtle
Left

Myrtle
Right

Water Iris

As the flower of roses in the spring of the year, as lilies of the rivers of the waters and as branches of the frankincense tree in the time of summer.
—Ecclesiasticus 50:8 (apocrypha)

The water iris, referred to as water lily (lilies palaestina), grew at the margins of ponds and streams, rivers and brooks, often in extensive masses. The iris has a delicate color of soft lemon and slight oxide blue. Iris is a Greek word for rainbow. In autumn, the bulb is uprooted and dried in the shade. The bulb has a delightfully pleasant odor and is placed in linen closets.

One young, innocent girl in one of my classes said, "Some of those wandering Arabs didn't have linens, so what did they do with the bulb?"

Another student answered, "If they stick it under their saddles, the camels will smell better!"

Project Specifications

Wall Quilt Size: 17 1/4" x 17 1/4"

Water Iris
14 1/4" x 14 1/4" Block

Fabric & Batting

- Neutral background square 15 3/4" x 15 3/4"
- 1/3 yard yellow-and-orange print for border and appliqué
- Scraps of 3 green prints, marbleized yellow and marbled tan for appliqué
- 2 1/4 yards purchased or self-made green binding
- Backing 21" x 21"
- Batting 21" x 21"

Supplies & Tools

- Template material of choice
- Moss green 6-strand embroidery floss
- Appliqué thread of choice to match fabrics
- All-purpose thread to blend with fabrics
- 1 spool natural quilting thread

Instructions

1. Referring to photo for color suggestions, prepare templates and fabric for appliqué method of choice. Appliqué pieces on background square.

2. With 3 strands of moss green 6-strand embroidery floss, embroider roots extending from bulb as shown on pattern.

3. Trim background square to 14 3/4" x 14 3/4".

4. From yellow-and-orange print cut four strips 2" x 19". Sew one strip to each side of center square as in General Instructions. Miter corners. Trim to square.

5. Layer backing, batting and block, and baste. Quilt as desired.

6. Bind quilt to finish. ✳

Water Iris
Bottom right

Water Iris
Top right

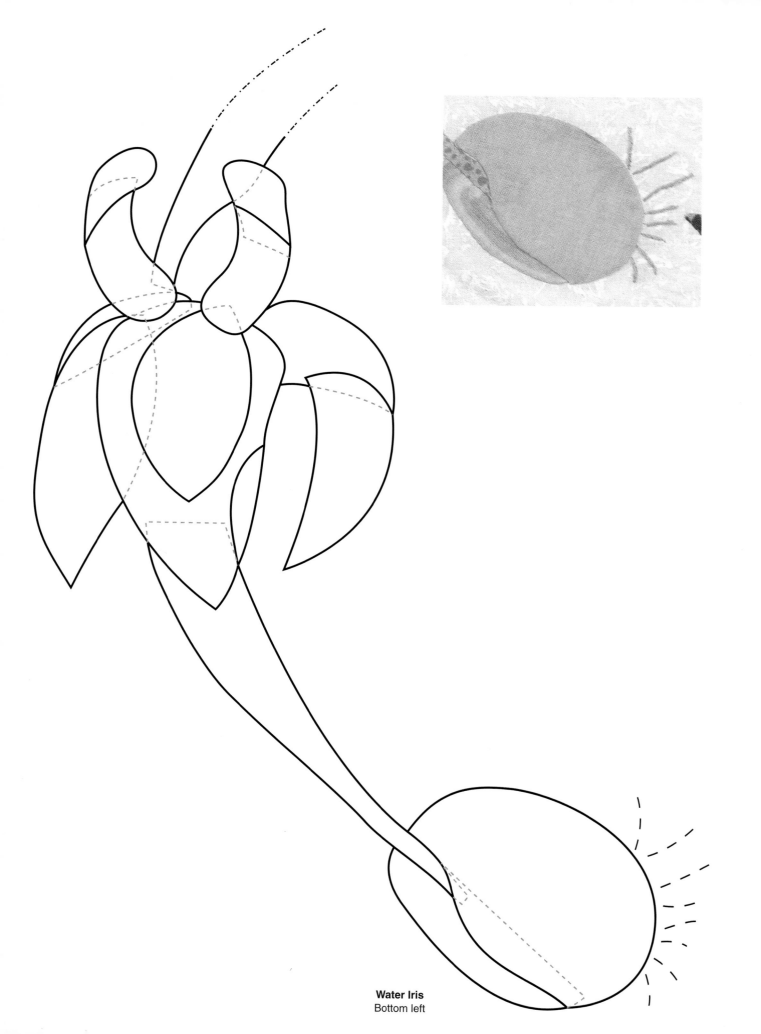

Water Iris
Bottom left

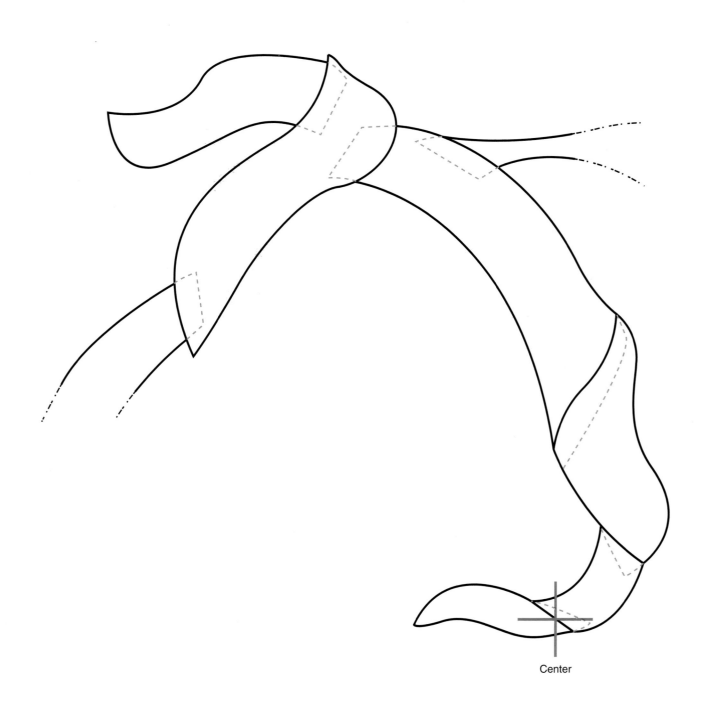

Center

Water Iris
Top left

Cockle
Top

Black Mustard

During biblical times, the mustard grew into a tree, enabling birds to nest in the upper branches. It is assumed that since there is no frost in the Holy Lands there was nothing to kill its growth.

We do not know if Jesus or the disciples had hair, because paintings that artists rendered were done many years after the crucifixion. But, we do know that mustard oil or seed, ground, was mixed with water and then applied to a bald head to encourage hair growth. If this process was successful, there is no record.

It was also advised that mustard could be used for snakebite, toothache and skin irritations.

Birds still enjoy eating mustard seeds.

Project Specifications

Wall Quilt Size: 18 3/4" x 18 3/4"

Fabric & Batting

- Neutral background square 16 1/2" x 16 1/2"
- 1/8 yard red print for center border and appliqué
- 1/4 yard yellow print for inner and outer borders and appliqué
- Scraps of red, yellow and green for appliqué
- 4 squares darker red print 2 3/8" x 2 3/8" for corner squares
- 2 1/4 yards purchased or self-made red binding
- Backing 23" x 23"
- Batting 23" x 23"

Supplies & Tools

- Template material of choice
- Appliqué thread of choice to match fabrics
- All-purpose thread to blend with fabrics
- 1 spool natural quilting thread

Instructions

1. Referring to photo for color suggestions, prepare templates and fabric for appliqué method of choice. Appliqué pieces on background square. Small leaves may be worked with reverse

Black Mustard
15" x 15" Block

appliqué if desired; see General Instructions.

2. Trim background square to 15 1/2" x 15 1/2".

3. From yellow print cut eight strips 1" x 15 1/2". From red print cut four strips 1 3/8" x 15 1/2". Sew a red strip between two yellow strips; press seams toward red strips. Repeat for four borders.

4. Sew one pieced border to two opposite sides of quilt. Sew one darker red print

2 3/8" x 2 3/8" square to each end of two remaining borders. Sew to top and bottom of quilt.

5. Layer backing, batting and block, and baste. Quilt as desired.

6. Bind quilt to finish. ✳

Center

Black Mustard
Left

Black Mustard
Right

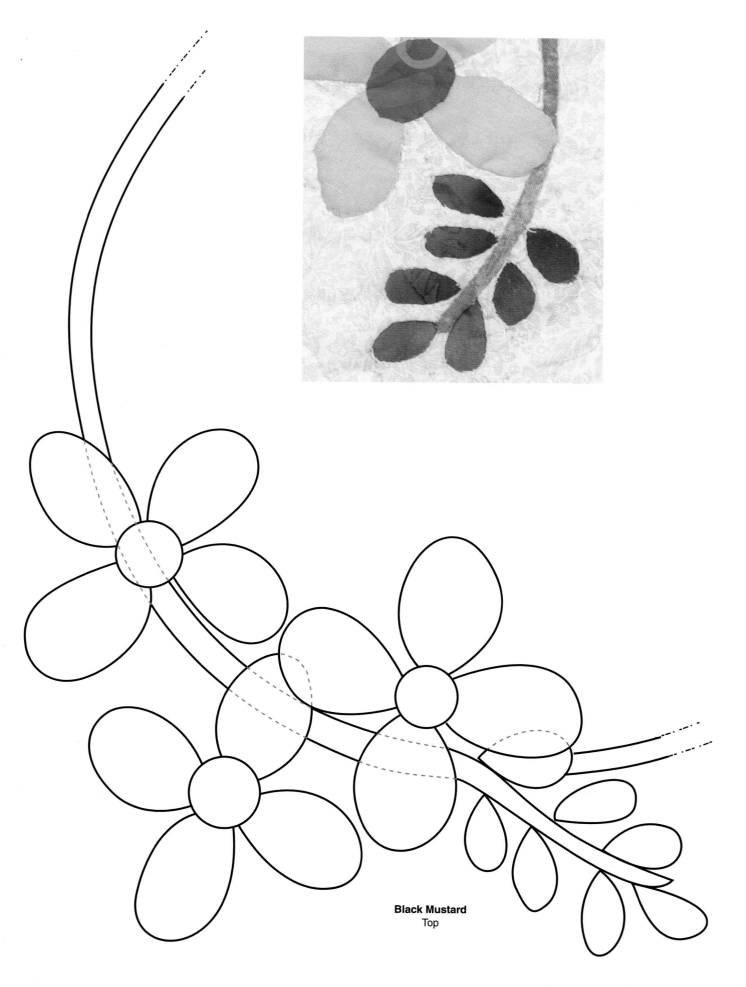

Black Mustard
Top

Crown of Thorns

And they clothed him with purple, and platted a crown of thorns, and put it about his head.
—Mark 15:17

Crown of thorns is another plant about which many have their own opinions. There are several species that could be considered. One grows 40 feet tall.

The final selection was the Christ Thorn, a straggling shrub 3–9 feet tall with zigzag branches, armed at the base of each leaf with spines—one straight and the other curved. The unusually pliable texture of the young branches renders it particularly easy to plait into a crownlike wreath.

The flowers, a soft cream color, are bisexual and produce drupes the size of cherries and are eaten and also marketed. The fruits are eaten by Arabs and have the taste of dried apples. The Arabs plant the shrub for shade. The Arabs revere the tree as sacred.

The thorn, today, is used for toothaches and tumors. The Lebanese believe all parts of the plant to be medicinal.

Crown of Thorns
14 1/4" x 14 1/4" Block

Project Specifications
Wall Quilt Size: 14 1/4" x 14 1/4"

Fabric & Batting
- Neutral background square 16" x 16"
- Scraps of green, brown, cream, yellow and gold for appliqué
- 1 3/4 yards purchased or self-made purple binding
- Backing 18" x 18"
- Batting 18" x 18"

Supplies & Tools
- Template material of choice
- Appliqué thread of choice to match fabrics
- All-purpose thread to blend with fabrics
- Green 6-strand embroidery floss
- 1 spool natural quilting thread

Instructions
1. Referring to photo for color suggestions, prepare templates and fabric for appliqué method of choice. Appliqué pieces on background square.
2. With 3 strands of green 6-strand embroidery floss, embroider veins on leaves and stems on drupes with stem stitch. Work stem stitch around outer edge of leaves, making two-stitch projections for thorns as shown on pattern.
3. Trim background square to 14 3/4" x 14 3/4".
4. Layer backing, batting and block, and baste. Quilt as desired.
5. Bind quilt to finish. ✳

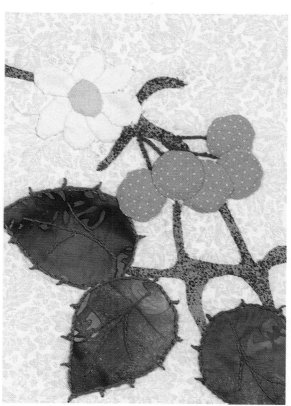

Crown of Thorns
Bottom

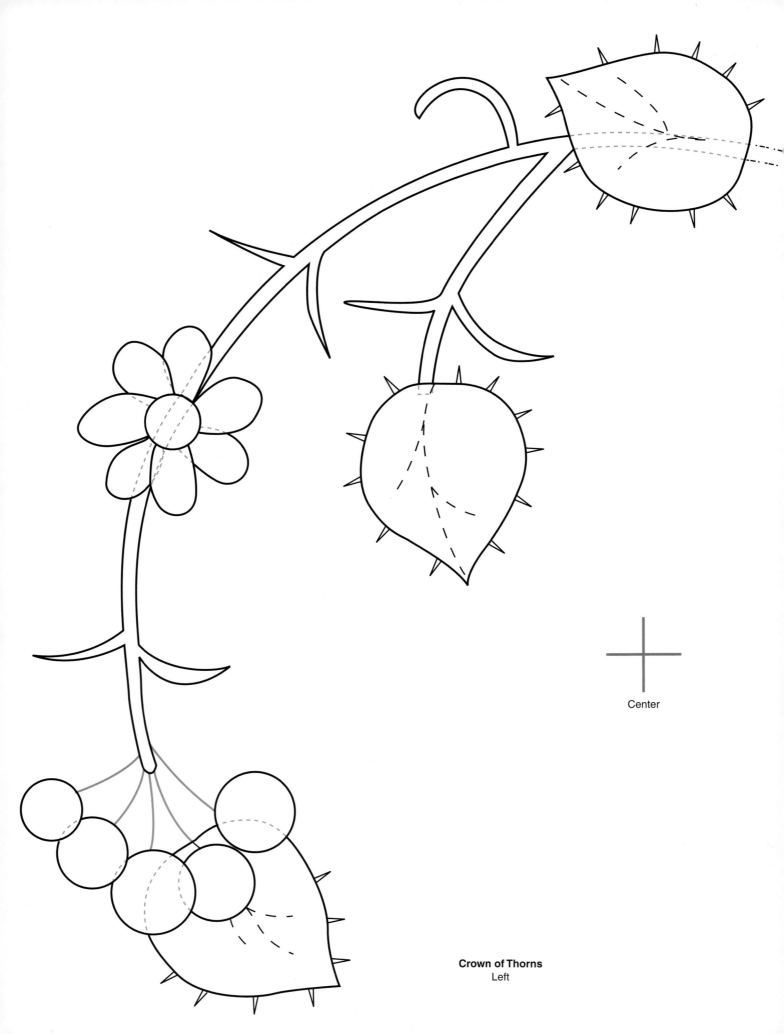

Crown of Thorns
Left

Center

Crown of Thorns
Top

Common Rue

But woe unto you, Pharisees!
For ye tithe mint and rue and all
manner of herbs, and pass over
judgment and the love of God:
these ought ye to have done, and
not to leave the other undone.

—Luke 11:42

Rue is only mentioned once in the Bible, although it was and is a very valuable herb.

In biblical times people drank honeyed wine flavored with rue. Leaves were scattered about courts of justice to protect officers from the stench and fevers of prisoners brought to court from their jail cells.

Women ate leaves as a contraceptive. It fell into disuse when the ladies broke out in a rash that was difficult to heal.

Shakespeare called rue the "herb of grace," as it was used to get rid of body lice and other insects. The early Catholic Church used rue to repel demons and evil.

Rue was very highly thought of by ancient people as medicinal. It was considered an antiseptic and a deterrent of contagion. It was

also believed to deter maids from going "wrong" in love affairs. It was advised they eat it when tempted.

It was used as a seasoning, but was also used to heal bee stings, wasps, scorpions and snakebites. It prevented dizziness, dumbness, epilepsy, inflammation of the eyes, insanity and the "evil eye."

If gunflints were packed with rue, it was guaranteed the shot would eventually hit its mark.

Today rue is found in bitters, vermouth and nonalcoholic beverages, baked goods, candy, frozen dairy deserts, gelatins and puddings.

Project Specifications

Wall Quilt Size: 18 1/4" x 18 1/4"

Fabric & Batting

- Neutral background square 16 1/2" x 16 1/2"
- 1/8 yard green-and-brown print for center border
- 3/8 yard yellow print for inner and outer borders and appliqué
- Scraps of green, brown, gold and yellow print for appliqué
- 2 1/4 yards purchased or self-made green binding
- Backing 22" x 22"
- Batting 22" x 22"

Supplies & Tools

- Template material of choice
- Appliqué thread of choice to match fabrics
- All-purpose thread to blend with fabrics

Common Rue
15" x 15" Block

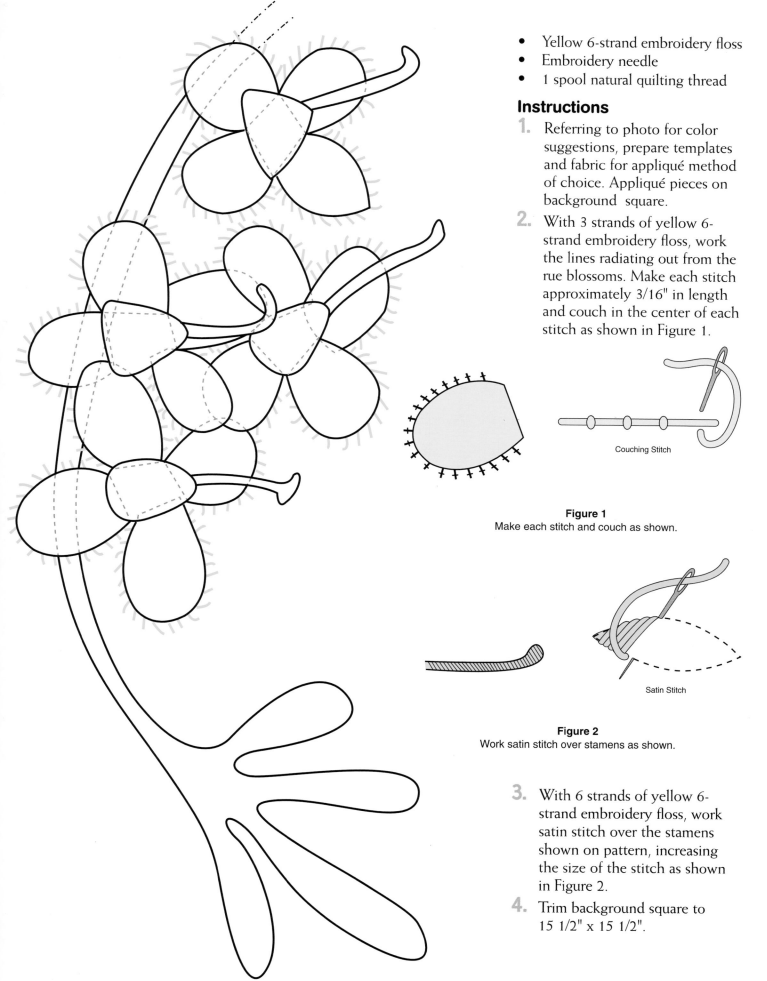

- Yellow 6-strand embroidery floss
- Embroidery needle
- 1 spool natural quilting thread

Instructions

1. Referring to photo for color suggestions, prepare templates and fabric for appliqué method of choice. Appliqué pieces on background square.

2. With 3 strands of yellow 6-strand embroidery floss, work the lines radiating out from the rue blossoms. Make each stitch approximately 3/16" in length and couch in the center of each stitch as shown in Figure 1.

Couching Stitch

Figure 1
Make each stitch and couch as shown.

Satin Stitch

Figure 2
Work satin stitch over stamens as shown.

3. With 6 strands of yellow 6-strand embroidery floss, work satin stitch over the stamens shown on pattern, increasing the size of the stitch as shown in Figure 2.

4. Trim background square to 15 1/2" x 15 1/2".

Common Rue
Left

5. From yellow print cut four strips each 1 1/4" x 22" and 1" x 22". From green-and-brown print cut four strips 7/8" x 22". Sew a green-and-brown strip between a yellow strip of each width. Press seams toward green-and-brown strips. Repeat for four borders. Handle each as a single border

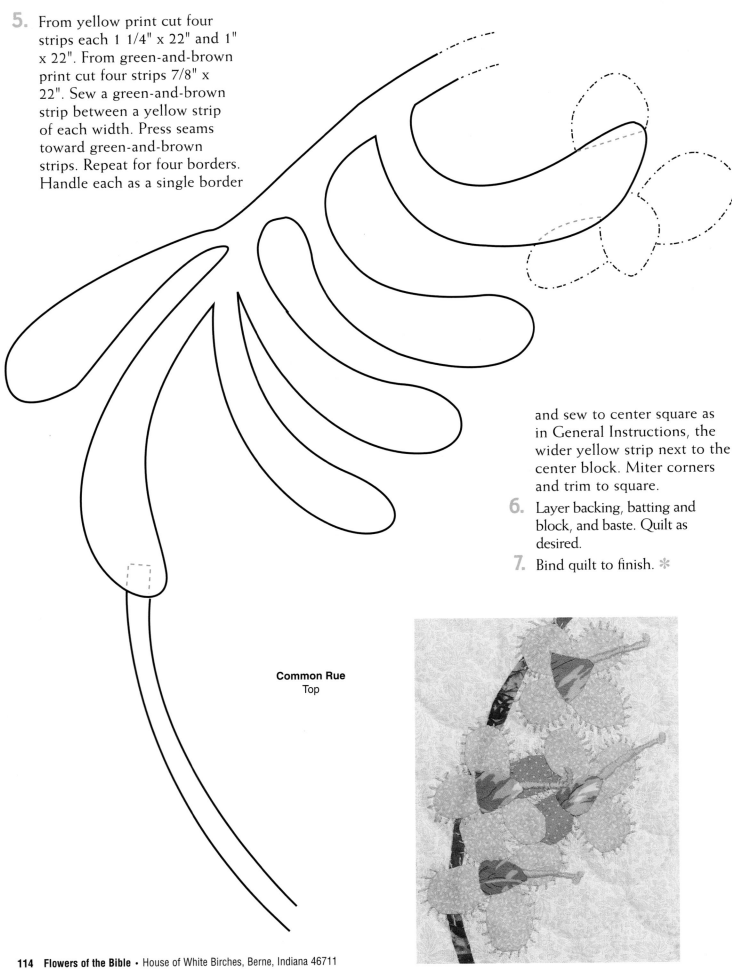

Common Rue
Top

and sew to center square as in General Instructions, the wider yellow strip next to the center block. Miter corners and trim to square.

6. Layer backing, batting and block, and baste. Quilt as desired.

7. Bind quilt to finish. ✳

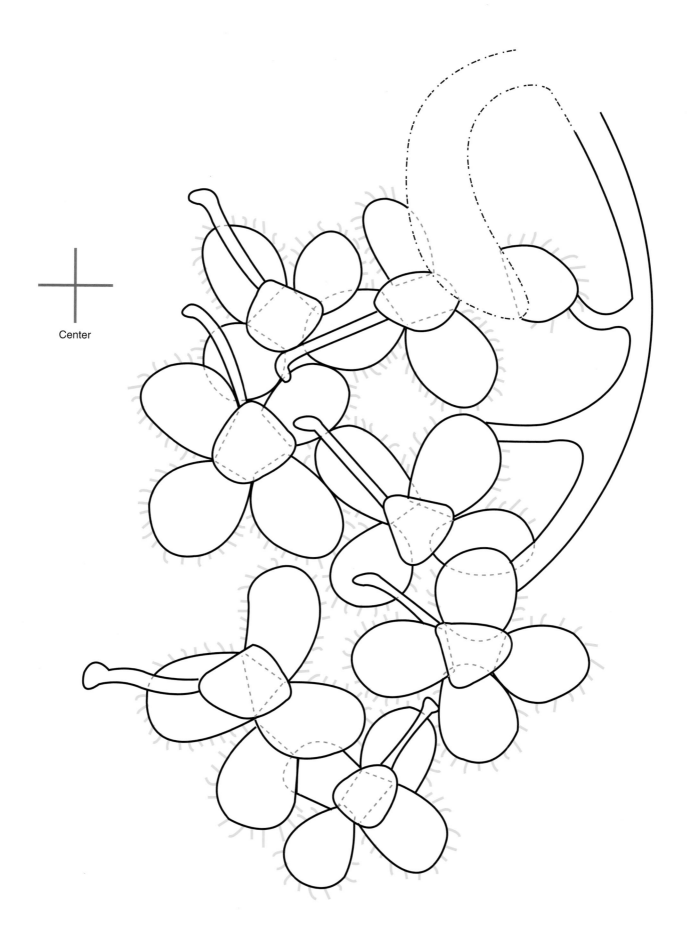

Center

Common Rue
Right

Aloe

And there came also Nicodemus, which at the first came to Jesus by night, and brought a mixture of myrrh and aloes, about an hundred pound weight.

—John 19:39

The aloe that we know today is not the same as from biblical times. At the time of Jesus' death, there was an aloe that had such a bitter smell that King Nicodemus neutralized it using 100 pounds of myrrh. Ancient Israelites washed their dead bodies with it. Probably they didn't know what smelled worse, the corpse or the aloe. Columbus, in 1492, remarked, "All is well, Aloes is on board."

People, for years, have grown aloe on their windowsills. If a cut leaf is dried out for having been left two weeks in the sun, it will rehydrate when soaked in water.

From biblical times to the present, the aloe is a giant among herbal medicines. Commercially we enjoy aloe bubble bath, lotions, soap and hand and body gels. It helps to heal skin irritations and burns. It is finding its way into cosmetics, emollients and shampoos.

Project Specifications

Wall Quilt Size: 20 1/2" x 19 "

Fabric & Batting

- Neutral background rectangle 17" x 15 1/2"
- 1/8 yard medium green mottled for center border
- 1/4 yard dark green print for inner and outer borders and appliqué
- Scraps of green, pink batik and gold solid for appliqué
- Scraps of pink, blue and green batik for corner squares
- 2 1/4 yards purchased or self-made dark green binding
- Backing 24" x 23"
- Batting 24" x 23"

Supplies & Tools

- Template material of choice

- Appliqué thread of choice to match fabrics
- All-purpose thread to blend with fabrics
- Green 6-strand embroidery floss
- Embroidery needle
- 1 spool natural quilting thread

Instructions

1. Referring to photo for color suggestions, prepare templates and fabric for appliqué method of choice. Appliqué pieces on background square, leaving opening at top of each pink batik blossom for folded gold-solid center.

2. Embroider around outer edges of aloe leaf with buttonhole stitch and 3 strands of green 6-strand embroidery floss. Reverse the direction of the stitch so the stitches extend onto the background as shown in Figure 1.

3. From gold solid scraps cut 12 squares 1" x 1". Fold each as shown in Figure 2 and insert

Aloe
15 1/2" x 14" Block

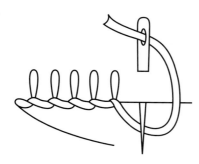

Figure 1
Reverse direction of buttonhole stitch so stitches extend onto background as shown.

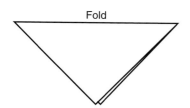

Fold

Figure 2
Fold 1" squares as shown.

Fold   Fold

one in the end of each pink batik blossom. Stitch in place.

4. Trim background rectangle to 16" x 14 1/2".

5. From dark green print cut four strips each 1 1/4" x 16" and 1 1/4" x 14 1/2". From medium green mottled cut two strips each 1 1/2" x 16" and 1 1/2" x 14 1/2". Sew one medium green strip between two dark green strips of same length. Repeat for four borders.

6. From green, pink and blue batik scraps cut 16 strips 1 1/8" x 3". Piece four strips together randomly as shown in Figure 3. Repeat for four corner blocks.

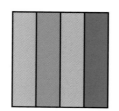

Figure 3
Piece 4 strips randomly as shown.

7. Sew two short borders to two opposite sides of quilt. Sew one corner square to each end of two remaining borders. Corner block stripes should run perpendicular to border stripes. Sew to top and bottom of quilt.

8. Layer backing, batting and block, and baste. Quilt as desired.

9. Bind quilt to finish. ✳

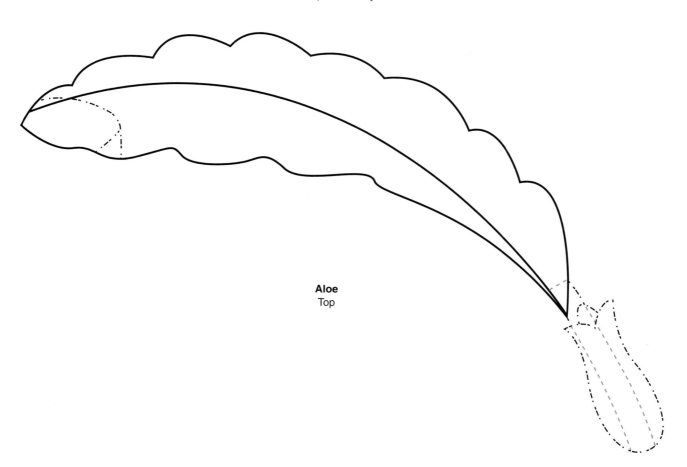

Aloe
Top

Aloe
Right

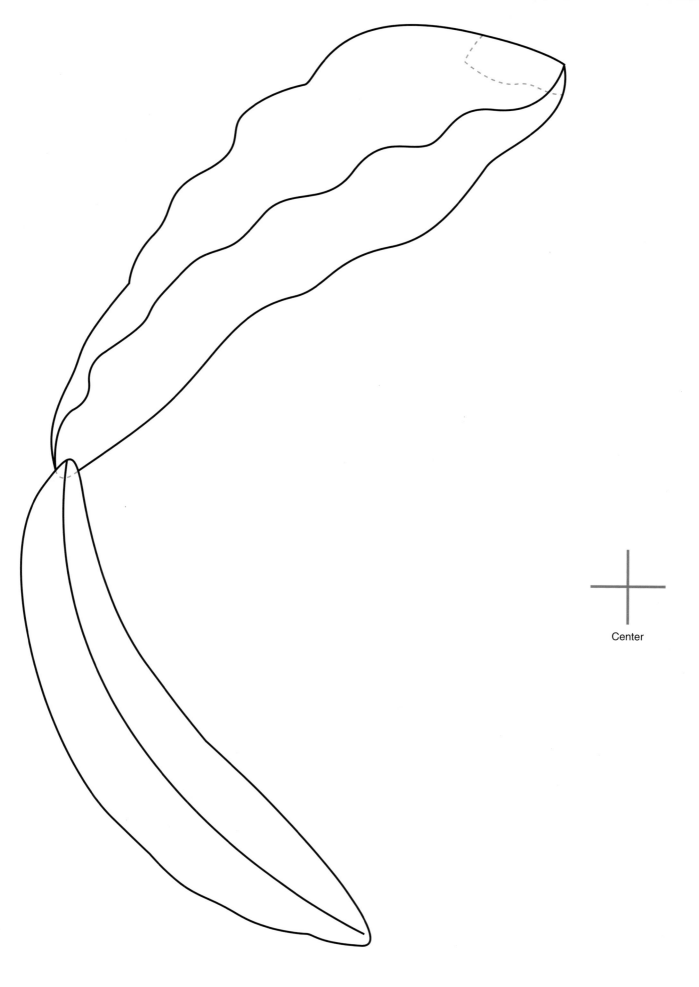

Center

Aloe
Left

Hyssop

After this, Jesus knowing that all things were now accomplished, that the scripture might be fulfilled, saith, I thirst.

Now there was set a vessel full of vinegar: and they filled a sponge with vinegar, and put it upon hyssop, and put it to his mouth. When Jesus therefore had received the vinegar, he said, "It is finished;" and he bowed his head and gave up the ghost.

—John 19:28–30

There are many references in the Bible concerning the hyssop: Exodus 12:22; I Kings 4:33; Psalms 51:7 and Leviticus 14:4. It would appear that the plant was associated with cleaning. Hyssop was used to purify the homes of lepers.

Many people assumed that marjoram, a well-known garden plant in the herb category (hyssopus officinalis,) was the biblical plant. Their assumption was wrong. The hyssop, or reed, on which the sponge of vinegar (sour wine) was placed could not have been marjoram, which is too short, but must have been a dhura cane or stalk, a tall cereal known in Palestine as Jerusalem corn, with strong stems over six feet in height.

During the Middle Ages bathing was not popular. The hyssop was used as an herb to cover fetid odors. The floors were covered and mattresses stuffed with it.

The plant, as you can imagine, is aromatic. Dried leaves are used as a condiment in Palestine and Egypt. Hyssop is a member of the mint family.

Project Specifications

Wall Quilt Size: 17 1/2" x 17 1/2"

Fabric & Batting

- Neutral background square 16" x 16"
- 1/4 yard white batiste or voile for ruching
- 1/3 yard green-and-brown print for borders and appliqué
- Green scraps for appliqué
- 2 1/4 yards purchased or self-made brown binding
- Backing 21" x 21"
- Batting 21" x 21"

Supplies & Tools

- Template material of choice
- Appliqué thread of choice to match fabrics
- All-purpose thread to blend with fabrics
- Green and yellow 6-strand embroidery floss
- 1 spool natural quilting thread

Instructions

1. Referring to photo for color suggestions, prepare templates and fabric for appliqué method of choice. Appliqué pieces on

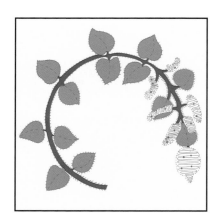

Hyssop
14 1/2" x 14 1/2" Block

background square.

2. Prepare white ruching strips for the areas marked with squiggles on the pattern by cutting 1 1/4"-wide strips across the width of the white batiste or voile. Repeat for as many strips as necessary to fill the areas. The actual length will depend on your stitching.

3. Fold under one end of strip 1/4"; press. Fold the strip in half along length with wrong sides together and press lightly to crease. Open strip. Fold the top long edge of the strip to meet the creased line on the wrong side of the strip as shown in Figure 1; press. Repeat with the bottom edge of the strip as shown in Figure 2.

Figure 1
Fold top edge of strip to creased line.

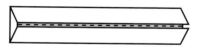

Figure 2
Fold bottom edge to creased line.

4. Using a knotted, doubled thread, bring your needle to the front of the strip at one corner. Stitch at an angle to the top edge of the strip with a long basting stitch;

turn and stitch at an angle to the bottom edge of the strip as shown in Figure 3. Repeat until you have made three V shapes; pull on the thread to gather as shown in Figure 4. Continue to stitch and gather along the length of the strip, stopping occasionally to place strip on background areas to measure for length. When correct length is completed, bring needle to back of strip on top edge; take several small stitches in one place to tie off. Trim length of strip if necessary; fold raw end to back of strip and stitch in place.

Figure 3
Stitch a V-shape as shown.

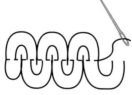

Figure 4
Pull thread to gather.

5. With 3 strands of green or gold (alternate colors) 6-strand embroidery floss, insert needle down through ruching strip and background square and back up. Tie knot on surface and trim close to

knot. Repeat as often as necessary to secure the ruching in place.

6. With 3 strands of green 6-strand embroidery floss, embroider leaf veins with stem stitch. Also work stem stitch around ruched areas to define.

7. Embroider around outer edges of leaves and stems with buttonhole stitch and 3 strands of green embroidery floss. Reverse the direction of the stitch so the stitches extend onto the background as shown in Figure 5.

8. Trim background square to 15" x 15".

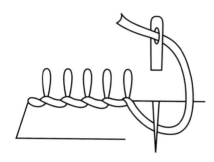

Figure 5
Reverse direction of buttonhole stitch so stitches extend onto background as shown.

9. From green-and-brown print cut four strips 2" x 19". Sew to center square as in General Instructions. Miter corners. Trim to square.

10. Layer backing, batting and block, and baste. Quilt as desired.

11. Bind quilt to finish. ✳

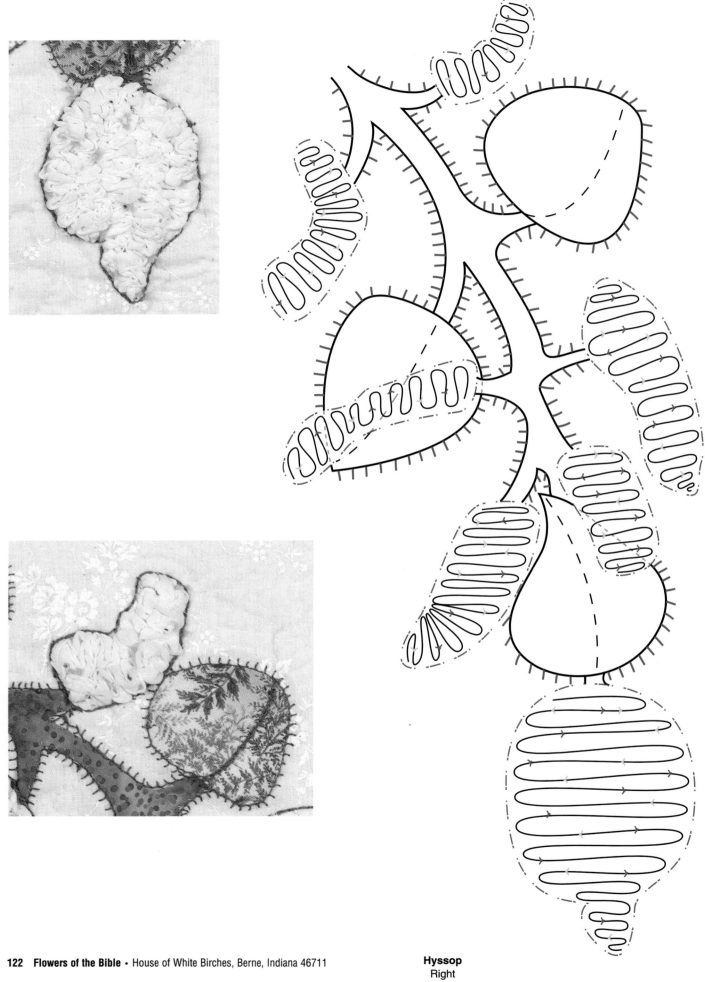

Hyssop
Right

Hyssop
Left

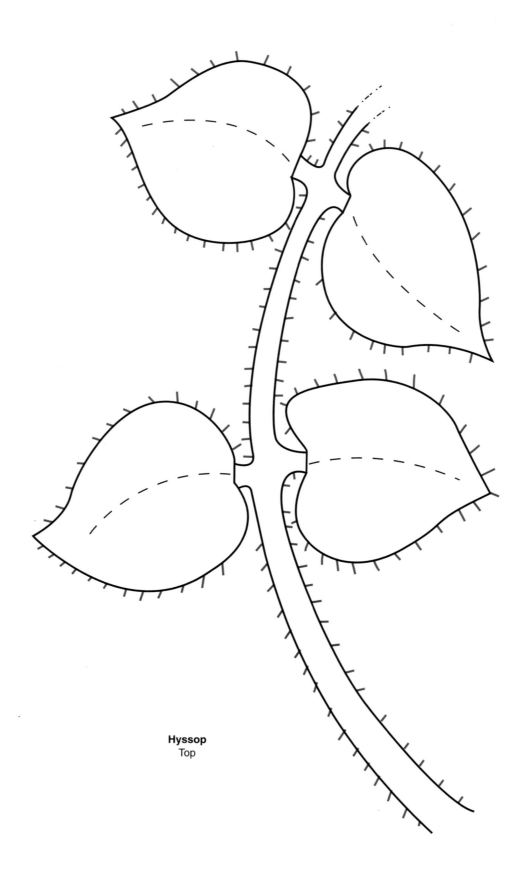

Hyssop
Top

General Instructions

Appliqué

Full-size patterns for the appliqué designs are included for each block in this book. Use your favorite method of hand or machine appliqué to complete the designs. Basic information and hints to help you successfully complete the blocks are given here. Read through these instructions before starting the blocks and refer to them as necessary. Any special instructions for a specific block are listed with the pattern. Embroidery floss color, strand number and stitches are also indicated with each block, if required. Refer to instructions for Embroidered Details on page 127 to complete the stitches.

Preparing Fabrics

You will need a background fabric, leaf fabrics and flower fabrics for each block. Refer to the Fabric & Batting list for fabric colors suggested for the block. You will also need lightweight fusible transfer web, fabric stabilizer and light-weight fusible interfacing if you choose to do machine appliqué.

Each block requires a neutral background fabric. Begin with the size required on the Fabric & Batting list, and after appliquéing the pieces trim to block size, plus seam allowances. A visually plain background allows the many small pieces of the flowers to stand out—tone-on-tone prints and mottled fabrics work well.

You will need a variety of small fabric pieces for the flower and leaf pieces. Tonal prints, batiks and subtle multicolor prints work well for the flower pieces and leaves. Use care with solid fabrics—the larger

pieces, such as leaves, will have no character without the shadings of the tonal prints or lines of the subtle prints. You may also find that solid fabrics will need additional embroidery for leaf veins or petal shadings to give them definition.

Minimal yardage will also be suggested for borders.

Press the background square. Lightly trace the pattern on the background square using a water-erasable marker or chalk pencil. Trace only enough lines to help place your pieces as shown in Figure 1; do not trace every detail of the pattern.

Figure 1
Trace only enough lines to place the pieces.

Refer to the photos of each block to select colors of each piece. Color matches do not need to be precisely the same, but analyze the contrast and shadowing of each piece for a pleasing result.

When preparing templates and pieces for either hand or machine appliqué, be sure to include the section of a piece that will be overlapped by an adjacent piece. This section is outlined with dashed lines on the pattern as shown in Figure 2.

Embroidery details are also included on the patterns and need to be

transferred to the templates and fabric pieces.

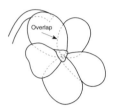

Figure 2
Overlapped sections are outlined with dashed lines.

Hand Appliqué

For traditional hand appliqué, prepare a finished-size template from plastic. Trace the plastic templates on the right side of selected fabrics, allowing about 1/2" between pieces as shown in Figure 3. Cut out the pieces, adding 1/8"–1/4" seam allowance to all edges, except those that will be overlapped by another piece. Turn under and hand-baste the seam allowance of each piece or leave seam allowances to needle-turn as you appliqué the pieces.

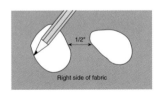

Figure 3
Trace plastic templates on the right side, leaving space between each piece.

Freezer Paper on the Back

For freezer-paper-on-the-back appliqué, photocopy or trace the design on a sheet of paper. Place the design side of the paper against a light box or bright window and trace the pieces on the paper side of freezer paper. Cut out the pieces on the traced lines. Press the freezer paper templates on the wrong side of the selected fabric with a hot, dry iron, leaving space between pieces as shown in Figure 4. Cut out the pieces, adding 1/8"–1/4" seam allowance to all edges, except those that will be overlapped by another piece. Press the seam allowance under using the edge of the freezer paper as a guide. Hand-baste in place through all layers to hold.

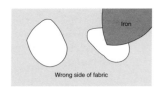

Figure 4
Press freezer-paper templates on the wrong side of fabric, leaving space between pieces.

Beginning with the underneath pieces and working toward the foreground, pin the pieces in place on the background, overlapping pieces as indicated on the pattern as shown in Figure 5.

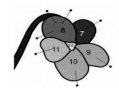

Figure 5
Pin the pieces in place, overlapping as necessary.

Blind-stitch the pieces in place, using thread to match the appliqué piece and turning under seam allowances, if necessary. Remove seam allowance basting.

To remove freezer paper, cut a small slit in the background behind each appliquéd piece as shown in

Figure 6. Remove the freezer paper piece using small tweezers.

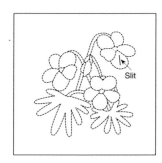

Figure 6
Cut a small slit in the background behind each appliquéd piece.

If darker pieces show through lighter top pieces, cut a slit through the background behind the darker piece and trim away the section of the darker piece that is overlapped by the lighter piece, leaving only a narrow seam allowance as shown in Figure 7. Trim the darker portion of the seam allowance, if necessary. Press the appliquéd design.

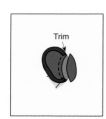

Figure 7
Trim dark fabrics overlapped by lighter fabrics.

Embroider any detail lines indicated on the pattern. The floss color, number of strands and stitches are given with the pattern. Refer to Embroidery Details on page 127 for stitch illustrations.

Trim the completed block to instructed size.

Freezer Paper on the Front

Trace the pattern pieces directly from the pattern onto the paper side of freezer paper. Cut out on

traced lines and with a hot, dry iron, press pieces to the right side of selected fabrics.

Cut out pieces, adding 1/8"–1/4" seam allowance to all edges, except those that will be overlapped by another piece. Trace around all edges with a fabric marker of choice. Remove freezer paper and pin or baste pieces to background, overlapping as indicated.

Needle-turn seam allowances, carefully including the traced line, as you blind-stitch in place.

Machine Appliqué

Fuse lightweight fusible interfacing to the wrong side of any light-color fabrics to prevent shadowing of darker fabrics.

Prepare a finished-size template from plastic for each piece in the design. Flip each template and trace the pieces to be cut from each fabric in a group on the paper side of lightweight fusible transfer web, leaving space between each fabric group as shown in Figure 8. Instead of making templates, you may photocopy or trace the pattern onto another sheet of paper. Place the design side against a light box or bright window and trace the pieces to be cut directly onto the fusible transfer web, again grouping each fabric's pieces.

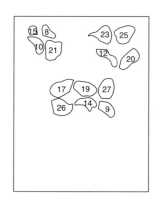

Figure 8
Trace pieces in groups by fabrics, leaving space between each group.

Roughly cut out each group of pieces, leaving a margin approximately 1/4" around each group. Fuse each group to the wrong side of the selected fabrics, following the manufacturer's instructions. Cut out each piece on the traced lines.

Beginning with the pieces farthest in the background, remove the paper backing and arrange the pieces on the background in ascending order, overlapping pieces as indicated on the pattern. When satisfied with the arrangement, fuse pieces to the background fabric.

You may find it easier to fuse small sections at a time of a pattern that has many pieces. Arrange one section in ascending order and fuse the pieces as shown in Figure 9. Move on to the next section and repeat. Continue fusing sections until the design is complete. Just remember to not only fuse the pieces within

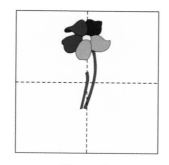

Figure 9
Arrange 1 section in ascending order

a section in ascending order, but to also fuse the pieces for the whole design in order. Otherwise, you may find that you have fused a piece in one section that should have overlapped a piece in another section.

Cut a piece of fabric stabilizer large enough to fit behind the fused design. Fuse or pin it in place on the wrong side of the background square.

Use all-purpose thread, machine-embroidery thread or rayon thread

to match each appliqué piece in the needle of your machine and all-purpose thread to match the background in the bobbin. Satin-stitch around the edges of each piece using a close medium-width stitch. Adjust your machine as necessary to prevent the bobbin thread from pulling to the top of your block.

Stitch detail lines indicated on the pattern. Use satin or straight stitches or other decorative machine stitches to complete the detail lines.

To hand-embroider the detail lines, refer to the special instructions given with the pattern for the floss color, number of strands of embroidery floss and the stitch to be used. Refer to Embroidered Details below for stitch illustrations.

Use a press cloth to press the appliquéd design. Trim the completed block to instructed size.

Embroidered Details

Embroidery is used to add details on many of the flower blocks. You may use machine or hand stitches to add these details. Special instructions for any embroidery are included for each block. These instructions include the floss color, number of strands of floss and stitches used in the block. Remember, every flower is not alike in nature, so you do not have to be concerned about stitching the exact number of French knots in your flower center or the same number of stamens as shown on the sample blocks.

Hand Embroidery

Use 6-strand embroidery floss in the color required for each detail. Cut an 18" length and separate into 6 individual strands. Rejoin the number of strands indicated for the pattern. Separating the strands helps to prevent knotting as you

stitch and gives more loft to your finished stitches.

Use a sharp, crewel embroidery needle. Thread the needle and make a small knot in one end of the length of floss.

Place the block section in a small embroidery hoop—a 5"–6" round hoop or 4 1/2" x 9" oval hoop is perfect. Do not over-tighten the hoop or pull on the block fabric to avoid excessive stress on the appliqué stitches.

Embroider the flower details using the stitch suggestions given with the block and referring to the stitch illustrations in Figure 1.

To make larger or smaller French knots, change the number of times you wrap the thread around the needle—more wraps make a larger knot; fewer wraps make a smaller knot.

Use a stem stitch to embroider leaf

veins and other detail lines.

Make small stitches under a stitched section or in an adjacent seam allowance section to end.

Machine Embroidery

Pin or fuse fabric stabilizer on the wrong side of the block under any areas to be embroidered. For an embroidery machine, prepare your block and place in the machine hoop following your sewing machine instructions.

Use all-purpose thread, machine-embroidery thread or rayon thread in the color required for each detail in the needle of your machine and all-purpose thread to match the block background in the bobbin. Use an embroidery sewing machine needle.

Lock your stitches at the beginning and end of each stitched detail line.

Use a straight stitch or narrow satin stitch for stamens, anthers and other straight lines. Use a narrow, very close zigzag stitch in place of French knots on the machine-appliquéd blocks. Use a decorative machine stitch for larger satin-stitched oval and round shapes. Remove fabric stabilizer, if necessary, when embroidery is completed.

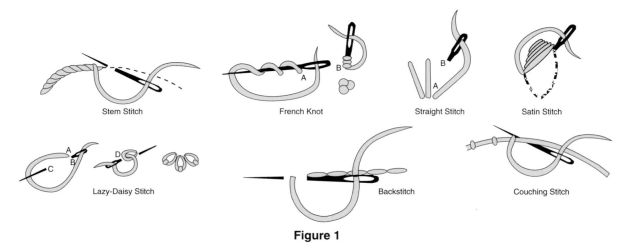

Figure 1

Finishing

The blocks in this book have been finished as single-block wall quilts. Most have multiple borders and mitered corners. Create the borders as instructed in each pattern, or create borders of your choice.

Borders

Trim the blocks to the size indicated on the pattern instructions.

Cut border strips as instructed. All are generously cut for ample length to miter corners.

Join the strips, if multiple colors and fabrics, and handle joined strips as a single border.

Find the center of each side of the block and mark. Find the center of the border and mark. Match the center of the border to the center of the block and pin in place.

Sew all four borders to the block, starting and stopping 1/4" from the corner and leaving the remainder of the strip dangling.

Press each corner at a 45-degree angle to form a crease as shown in Figure 1. Trim any additional border length even with the border. Stitch from the inside quilt corner

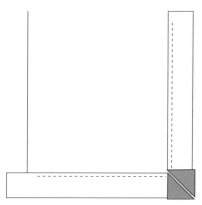

Figure 1
Fold and press corner to make a
45-degree angle.

to the outside on the crease line. Trim seam after stitching and press the mitered seams open as shown in Figure 2.

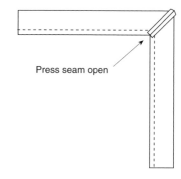

Figure 2
Trim stitched seam and press open.

Quilting

Refer to photos for quilting ideas. Appliqué shapes are often outline-quilted. If more than one row of outline stitches is used, it is called echo quilting. Evenly space the echo quilting rows around the design and continue to create the design in subsequent rows.

Sometimes quilting is done in the background, such as cross-hatch quilting, where straight lines cross each other at 90-degree angles on the background, but do not go through the appliqué shapes.

Other designs, such as the clam-shell pattern, are quilted in an allover design.

Fancy designs can be chosen for blocks, sashing and borders. These designs can be original, use everyday motifs such as circles or you may use designs especially created for quilting. There are many books and magazines filled with quilting designs.

Quilting designs should be marked on the quilt top before it is layered with backing and batting. A sharp, medium-lead pencil may be used on light background fabrics. Test the pencil marks to be sure they will wash out when quilting is complete, or be sure that your quilting stitches cover the line. Mechanical pencils with very fine points may also be used successfully to mark quilts.

Whatever marking tool you use should never show on the finished quilt.

Layering

Backing fabric and batting are usually cut about 4" larger than the quilt top. The Fabric & Batting list will give suggested sizes for each project.

Place the backing wrong side up on a flat work surface. Place the batting on the backing and smooth it carefully.

Place the quilt top on the batting and carefully smooth.

To hold the layers together for quilting, baste by hand or use safety pins. Safety pins work especially well for machine quilting.

Quilting

Quilting may be done by hand or by machine in the design of your choice.

Binding

Trim the backing and batting layers flush with the top of the quilt.

The list of materials for each project will include the amount of binding required. Bias binding may be purchased in packages and in many colors. Self-made binding often adds a nice coordinated finish to your quilt.

Double-fold, straight-grain binding is successfully used on small projects such as those in this book.

Cut the selected fabric in 2 1/2"-wide strips on the straight grain of the fabric. Join the strips as shown in Figure 3 to make binding of sufficient length.

Fold the binding lengthwise, wrong sides facing, and press.

Pin the folded binding along one edge of the quilt, starting in the

middle of one side and aligning the raw edges. Stitch, with a walking foot if you have one, to within 1/4" of the first corner; backstitch.

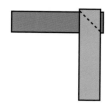

Figure 3
Join binding strips in a diagonal seam as shown.

Turn the quilt; fold the binding at a 45-degree angle up and away from the quilt as shown in Figure 4. Fold the binding back down, flush with the raw edge of the quilt as shown in Figure 5. Repeat at each corner as you stitch around the quilt.

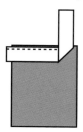

Figure 4
Fold binding at a 45-degree angle up and away from quilt.

Figure 5
Fold binding back down flush with raw edge of quilt.

As you approach the beginning of the binding strip, stop stitching and overlap the binding 1/2" from the edge; trim. Join the two ends with a 1/4" seam allowance and press the seam open. Reposition the joined binding along the edge of the quilt and resume stitching to the beginning.

To finish, bring the folded edge of the binding over the raw edges of the quilt and blind-stitch the folded edge of the binding in place over the machine-stitching line of the backside.

Topography of the Holy Lands

The Holy Land is only 150 miles long and the climate is extremely varied. This area is unequaled by any other country or area of the same size in the world in it´s diversity of surface and climate, which permits so many different species of flora and fauna to exist.

The mountains of Lebanon rise 10,500 feet. The climate is extremely cold, almost arctic, while the lower portion of the Jordan Valley is tropical.

There is a distinct western coastal area with sand dunes, lush meadows and a region of inland plains and foothills. There are surrounding deserts of Syria, South and Southwest Arabia, the Sinai Peninsula and Egypt.

The barrenness and desolation of so much of the area today has two causes. First, the cutting down of all the natural timbers by the natives and by successive hordes of invaders from 705–681 B.C to A.D. 70, leaving the area stripped of topsoil. Sound familiar? Remember our Dust Bowl?

Originally the area was a rich land; a land of brooks and fresh water, of deep fountains that sprang out of the hills and valleys. It was a land where residents could eat bread without concern of scarcity. According to Deuteronomy 8:7–8, Jeremiah 12: 10 and Malachi 3:12, this area was pleasant and productive.

Centuries of misrule and neglect combined with natural avenging forces transformed this natural paradise into a desolate area.

The winter rains swept the remaining thin soil from the hillsides. The peasants demolished both forest and fruit trees, never giving a thought to replanting. Thus, most of the springs ran dry. Streams fed pestilential marsh and the thorn plant and thistles took over.

Parts of the biblical regions are some of the worst stark testimonials of soil erosion and land exploitation. It would seem that the promised land of 3,000 years ago is a myth and never existed.

Colors in the Bible

The Bible places deep significance on color.

Blue

Truth is revealed under a clear blue sky. Blue is the color of Mary. Dark blue indicates richness; blue is the color of baptismal waters and heavens, and blue was chosen by the Israelites to depict the Star of David.

And every wise hearted man among them that wrought the work of the tabernacle made ten curtains of fine twined linen, and blue, and purple, and scarlet: with cherubims of cunning work made he them.
—Exodus 36:8

Yellow

Yellow means two-sided; cowardice. Felons' and traitors' doors were painted yellow in France. Yellow is the color of sun and gold; light of God.

Though you have lien among the pots, yet shall ye be as the wings of a dove covered with silver, and her feathers with yellow gold.
—Psalms 68:13

Green

Green symbolizes the triumph of spring over winter, fertility, hope, jealousy, the Irish and their nation.

He maketh me to lie down in green pastures: he leadth me beside the still waters.
—Psalms 23:2

Red

Red signifies the power and blood of the martyrs, love and hate, fires of faith and of Pentecost. Red-letter days were when saints' feast days were printed in red on calendars.

And the rams' skins dyed red, and badgers' skins, and shittim wood.
—Exodus 25:5

Purple

Purple means loyalty, toga color of the Roman Emperor, predominant penance and fasting Lenten celebration.

And a certain woman named Lydia, a seller of purple, of the city of Thyatira.
—Acts 16:14

Black

Black indicates evil, darkness, loss of sun, and later, loss of the light provided by the Son of God.

And it came to pass in the meanwhile that the heaven was black with clouds and wind.
—I Kings 18:45

White

White is purity, truth, innocence and the original color of mourning replaced by black. Druid priests wore white and sacrificed white bulls.

Come now, and let us reason together, said the Lord: though your sins be as scarlet, they shall be as white as snow; though they be red like crimson, they shall be as wool.
—Isaiah 1:18

Bibliography

Anderson, A.W. *Plants and Civilization.* Belmont, Calif.: 1965.
Duke, James S. *Medicinal Books of the Bible.* Trado-Medic Books.
Fauna and Flora of the Bible. London: United Bible Societies.
Grant, William C. *Video Secrets of the Pharaohs.*
King, E.A. *Bible Plants for America.* New York: Dover Publishing.
Moldenke, A.L. and H.N. *Plants of the Bible.* New York: Ronald Press Co.
Paterson, Wilma. *A Fountain of Gardens; Plants and Herbs of the Bible.* Overlook Publishers.
Patterson, John. *Consider the Lilies; Plants of the Bible.* Crowell, N.Y.: John Barstow Publisher.
Rabinowitz, Louis T. *Torah and Flora.* New York: Sanhedrin Press.
Rooted in Spirit; Exploring Inspirational Gardens. Taylor Publishing.
Sienkiewicz, Elly. *Baltimore Beauties and Beyond.* Lafayette, Calif.: C&T Publishing.
Sienkiewicz, Elly. *Dimensional Appliqué.* Lafayette, Calif.: C&T Publishing,
Sienkiewicz, Elly. *The Best of Baltimore Beauties.* Lafayette, Calif: C&T Publishing, 2000.
Smit, D. *Plants of the Bible: A Gardener's Oxford England.* Taylor Publishing.
The Flowers and Fruits of the Bible. New York: Beauforsts Books Inc.
The Holy Bible: The Clear Word Reference Edition. Royal Publishers.
Walker, Winifred. *All the Plants of the Bible.* Harper & Bros. Publishing.
Whittemore, Carroll E. *Symbols of the Church.* Abington Press.
Wilder, L.B. *The Fragrant Gardens; About Sweet Scented Leaves and Flowers.* New York: Dover Publishing.
Zohary, Michael. *Plants of the Bible.* Cambridge.